Neil Spiller Lost Architectures

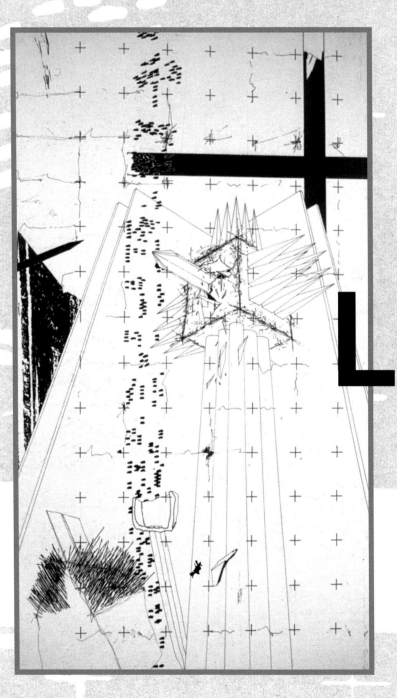

Lost

Architectures

Neil Spiller

WILEY-ACADEMY

ACKNOWLEDGEMENTS

Neil Spiller would like to thank all the architects who have given their work and thoughts of yesteryear so freely. For some, it has been like digging up dinosaurs.

This book is dedicated with love to Melissa and Edward.

Cover: CJ Lim, Mark Smout, Dominique Leutwyler, Rachel Calladine, Architecture Centre, Newcastle, 1995.
Frontispiece: Kevin Rhowbotham, Conceptual Sketch, 1984.
Page 128: A postcard picturing a Ben Nicholson made model of a Libeskind scheme and on reverse a Nicholson note to the young Jesse Reiser.

First published in Great Britain in 2001 by Wiley-Academy

A division of
JOHN WILEY & SONS
Baffins Lane
Chichester
West Sussex PO19 1UD

ISBN 0–417–49535–2

Other Wiley Editorial Offices
New York, Weinheim, Brisbane, Singapore, Toronto

Cover design: Artmedia Press, London
Designed and typeset by Florence Production Ltd, Stoodleigh, Devon
Printed and bound in Italy

Contents

Lost architectures:
visions of splendour

The less insightful architectural histories tracing the last two decades of the twentieth century would wager that this period will be remembered for late Modernism, the flowering of High-tech and the brief abomination of architectural Postmodernism, with a bit of folding, deconstruction and topological morphosis thrown in. But this view is too easy, too exclusive and panders too much to the establishment. *Lost Architectures* seeks to excavate some of the more esoteric, idiosyncratic and iconoclastic work of the late twentieth century; *fin de siècle* architectural decadence, one might say.

How do we lose architectural projects? Architects are educated on dreams and optimism, but the architect's lot is often one of extreme effort and ultimate disappointment. Disappointment because of the job that got away, the fruitlessness of competitions, or the sad, serene beauty of the stillborn student thesis or theoretical project. In a sense, to build is to admit failure, to cast beautiful ideas to the dogs of capitalism and the inertia of specification and budget. Some will tell you that the only true architecture is built on compromise. This is hogwash.

This book tells the missing part of the story of architecture at the end of the second millennium. It contains work that was influential at the time but did not get its authors knighthoods, urban task forces, RIBA gold medals, well-heeled clients, or large bucks. Often, the flow of capital has never wetted the projects discussed here; it has sometimes licked them a little bit but ultimately ignored them. It is mostly unfettered by the computer – in many cases it is the last hand-drawn work of the architects, and therefore still maintains its visceral immediacy.

In academic circles, people become obsessed with the 'criteria of assessment' of architectural work. It might be useful to state mine for this book. Firstly, I liked the work at the time; secondly, I still like it; thirdly, it is not as well published as it should be; fourthly and finally, it is brave. Above all, I value bravery, originality and bloody minded achievement, whether it is in seeing the heroic drawing through to the end, or in dancing with unfamiliar ideas, or in expanding the limitations of architectural discourse. These, then, are the parameters that mould my appreciation of the work in this book. It is not meant to be exhaustive – it is just as exclusive as all other histories and just as prejudiced as all other histories. It is an offering that might be seen as an antidote to High-tech giants, postmodern demons and decon divas.

After the summer of Punk, the Sex Pistols' river trip, for a whole generation, my generation, nothing was ever the same again. This was a generation of iconoclasts, a generation of choice, a generation *demanding* choice – above all, hedonistic choice – a generation caught in an internalised selfish spectacle. The work featured here emerges from this extraordinarily diverse and fecund period, when, for some, what was seen as the architectural *Zeitgeist* was not loose enough, succulent enough, thrilling enough, nor theatrical enough.

At the beginning of the 1980s, Modernism was pronounced in good health by most commentators. But in small enclaves and niches (it must be said mostly in London) it was not getting the sort of house room it was used to. In fact, it was often pushed out of the door into the acid rain where it huddled defensively, offering little to recommend itself apart from capitalist self-righteousness. In my opinion, it never recovered; it never came in from the cold.

As Peter York, the self-styled style guru, commented to an Architectural Association audience sometime in 1981:

> In the midst of all withdrawal, there is the ongoing theme – modern, deluded, nutty, romantic – of the search for Authenticity. In the midst of the pastiche, people look for Authenticity. They're dead-set on the Authenticity trail, looking for experience ripped live from the carcass. I really do think that is why those American shock-horror films are so much a part of high culture now. The search for Authenticity along with technical withdrawal, and the acceptance that neither is completely the answer, but living quite comfortably with the contradictions . . . [1]

Caught between the poles of the glorification of technology for its own sake, pastiche, and purity of functional form, was a virulent type of architectural perversity. Its beginning was shaky, sketchy and masked within an existing modernist rant. But it gestated into a confident, mature and diverse body of work that now seems to have been left by the wayside, replaced by the technological imperative, late Modernism, and a sort of a playschool art aesthetic that sees the popular as unequivocally good.

EM Farrelly, in a seminal issue of *Architectural Review*, 'The New Spirit', describes this tendency:

> It began honourably enough. Modernism may have been heroic, but it never won the affection of the public. By the 1970s, widely misinterpreted and misapplied, it had become brittle and diagrammatic; the revolution when it came was driven by a craving for liberation from its strictures, both moral and aesthetic. Postmodernists, in those early days seemed like freedom fighters, dragon slayers, and heroes . . . The New Spirit can be strange, wilful, even at times subversive, but it is unfailingly vigorous, exploratory and although it takes no heed of fashion, very much an architecture of *now*.[2]

Whether or not one agrees with this hypothesis, there was certainly something in the air. Most of the architects in this book, however, were not part of the 'New Spirit' thing. Perhaps a more fitting description for many of those within these pages is, oddly, 'New Romantic'. The New Romantic project was sometimes camp, sometimes posey, sometimes made a great deal of effort to do something relatively simple. It had a healthy liking for aesthetic decadence, fey mannerism, shaggy angularity and mechanised ritual. Peter Cook once called the brutalist organicism of early Webb and Outram 'the lost movement of Bowellism'. Though I do not seek to pigeonhole these architects, nor to invent a new style, I would like the reader to consider this book to be about the lost movement of New Romanticism. It is a romanticism that is sometimes caught up with middle-class slumming, interest in the found object, the spaces of events, and patina and decay. It is sometimes figurative, sometimes narrative; a rampant modernist would dismiss it as morally nonchalant.

This book is a resource for students of architecture – those still studying and those who follow its form. It contains documentary evidence of the existence of something else, something that had a vitality of its own and the arrogance to clothe itself flamboyantly. Its proponents are still out there, waiting, I hope, poised and ready. Some are even actually building!

Notes

1   Peter York, 'Style Wars', *AA Files*, no 1, Architectural Association, Winter 1981–2.

2   EM Farrelly (ed), 'The New Spirit', *Architectural Review*, August 1986.

Opposite: Ben Nicholson, Grunewald House, 1980. Elemental studies.

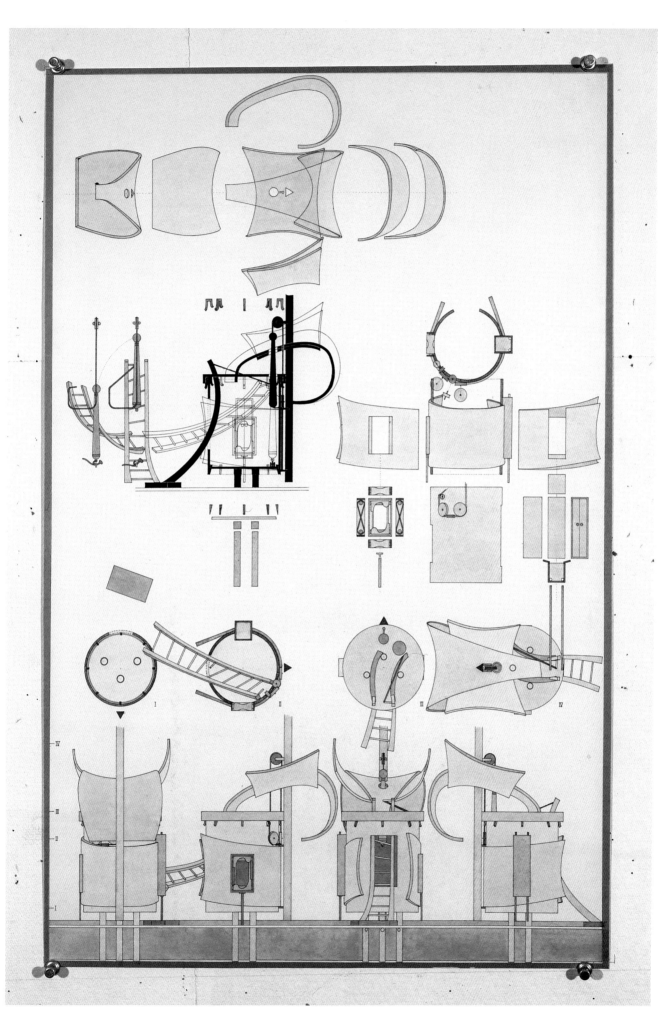

Tuning the device

Andrew Yeoman – T151

During the mid-1980s, one of the most innovative practices to emerge on the London architectural scene was T151. Its work was characterised by a certain compositional strength in section and an ability to concoct an aesthetic motif within each project. This motif determined a specific, recognisable aesthetic for each project, whether it was conditioned by a careful re-evaluation of the figure and ground or the sectional part. Sectionally, T151's work seldom revealed the rigid, simple layering of space, but attempted a more ambitious complexity. Additionally, T151 was and still is a collaborative practice; it seeks connections with other designers and works with them to mutual benefit.

Why T151? The practice is named after a stumpy tower on London's Smithfield meat market: Tower 151. This was the home of its first studio, above 'Sid's Sausages' – 'The purveyor of the best sausages in London', I was once told by a cab driver. In the early 1990s, Smithfields was a rundown area of London. Today, it is a trendy centre for architectural offices, publishers and authors' agents.

 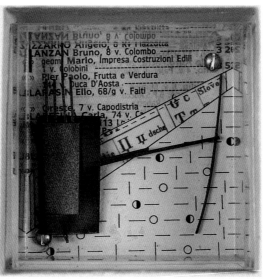

This page and opposite: Conceptual device collages.

10

Tuning the device
Andrew Yeoman

What was immediately obvious was that T151's frontman, Andrew Yeoman, displayed a strong architectural eye – that mystical quality that singles out a good designer. The work was delicate, finely articulated, compositionally elegant and dynamic.

At the end of the 1980s, the bottom fell out of the domestic market for architectural services, and T151, like most young practices at the time, was forced to look for pastures new. Simultaneously with the burn-out of the Western economies, Eastern Europe was in turmoil after the fall of the Berlin Wall. This new urban potential attracted quite a number of the more mobile practices. Few had the guts to move there, but T151 went to Zagreb in Croatia, which was not only in a state of economic turmoil but also terribly marred by ethnic division and war. These were stark and hungry times for cities and architects alike. T151 collaborated with many local architects and officials to attempt to create new urban models that took advantage of the changes to the local economy yet did not indulge in the crass 'ambulance chasing' of so many well-known architectural practices. This 'on-the-ground' contact allowed T151 to be much more sensitive, proactive and responsive to local need. To date, an impressive array of urban proposals has been conducted.

Of T151's early work, Georgi Stanishev wrote:

> In the 1980s the writings and architecture of T151 showed a general tendency to research the impartial correlations able to link ideology to expression, sense to speculation, form to reason, etc. This attempt led to the specific concept of urban device, then understood as a transition mechanism mediating between the urban conditions in different moments of their evolution and the structure of the design proposal.[1]

Though the scale of T151's work has grown over the years, its propositions still utilise this notion of the device as a conceptual tool. Each project has a different device or series of devices, developed by the peculiar conditions of space and time that face the architects at a given point in the city. These devices are instrumental in creating a conversation between aspects of the context or design. As T151 puts it:

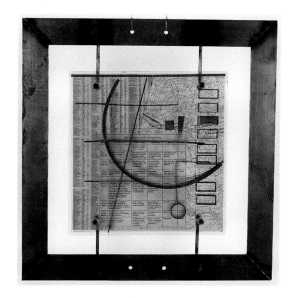

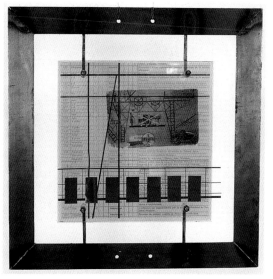

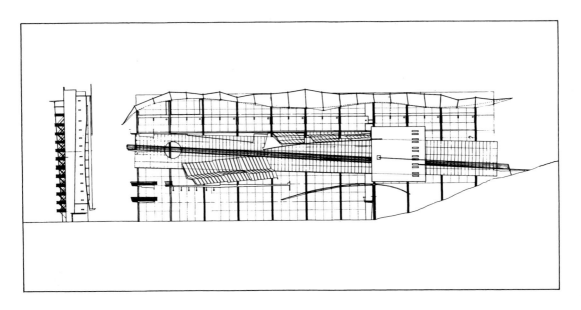

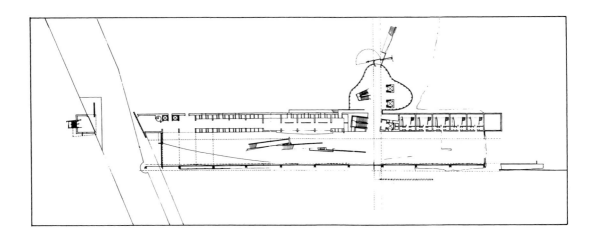

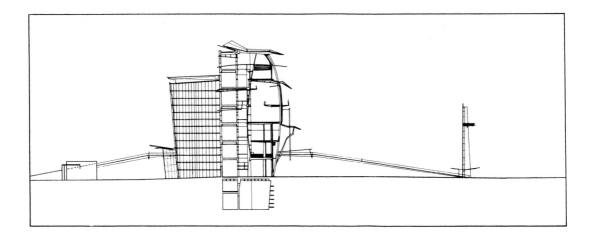

Gorizia/Nova Gorica, Border Library, 1991. From the top: elevation facing Gorizia; ground floor plan; section.

Tuning the device
Andrew Yeoman

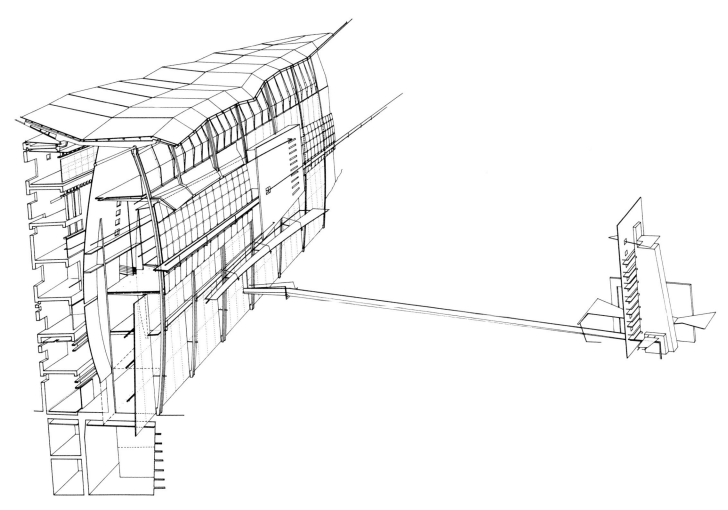

Gorizia/Nova Gorica, Border Library, 1991. Sectional perspective.

The tools and means we employ as architects generate a certain 'signature'. These signs and identifying codes may be read by the observer and perhaps interpreted in ways not considered by the authors. The tools themselves are, however, mute, often discarded. Devices that serve and yet disappear. In some way to remedy this situation, and experiment with hidden possibilities, we identify with sensibilities, which are, by theoretical proclivities, philosophical leaning etc, embedded in the work. Evidence of the manufacturing processes will be manifest in the determined result of building.[2]

This is true of two projects in particular: the mediating tower devices of Gorizia\Nova Gorica and the Glasgow Tower, both designed in the

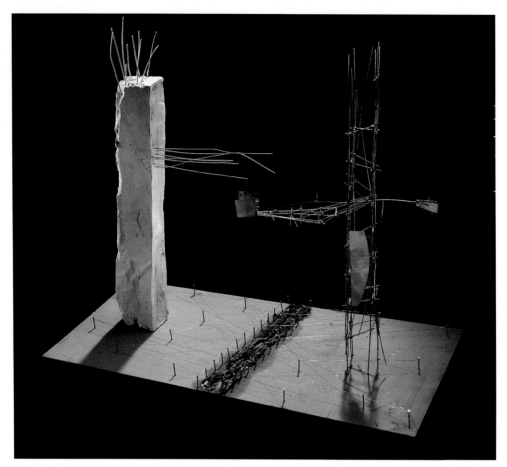

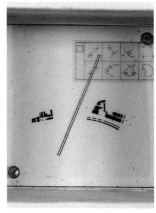

Gorizia/Nova Gorica, 1991.
Conceptual model and
conceptual drawing of
boundary conditions.

early 1990s. T151 has become acutely aware of the impact of boundary conditions on politics and architecture:

> Observation of Gorizia and Nova Gorica focused on a common demographical condition in a variegated urban pattern; an analysis that may be considered as reconciliation. After forty years of separation in which two systems have evolved, the cultures which coexist have nevertheless left the border naked, a line on a map . . . Through the initial studies of figure-ground, a focus on the two sites either side of the border through differing filters of geometry, spatial relationships and culture, revealed a constant: that of the border. We then considered the union of these sites; a weave of social paths provided a matrix of activity, the kernel of which was found in and on the border.

> By proposing the placing of a new library on this line or border we established a line to be centre, not bisection or a line for lateral transgression. The object becomes the protagonist . . .[3]

The Glasgow Tower was firmly within international boundaries but was iconographic in another way:

> This tower in Glasgow is proposed as a celebration of all the elements of progress with its height being reciprocated by its depth, where chambers are situated in which historical and cultural aspects of Glasgow can be viewed. In glass chambers above ground, the earth and artefacts from the excavation are held . . .[4]

T151 continuously attempts to create positions relative to the full gamut of urban, political and philosophical conditions between and within sites and countries. Yet engaging with these larger issues has not censored its obvious joy in the knowing curve or the naughty cantilever. It aims to drag the more fun sides of Modernism – the Situationists' *Derive*, or De Stijl, for example, into the twenty-first century fray.

Notes

1   *Tower 151 Architects* (exhibition catalogue) Arkitekturgalleriet 6, Dansk Arkitektur Center, 1998.

2   Ibid.

3   Ibid.

4   Ibid.

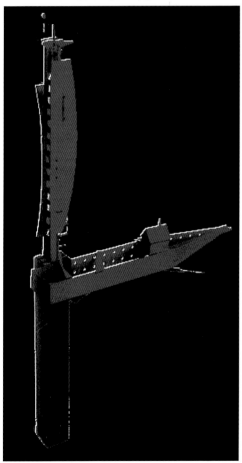

Glasgow Tower, 1990.

Techno-rusticity

Martyn Wiltshire

During the mid-1980s, some of the most interesting work coming out of the Architectural Association in London seemed, on the face of it, to represent two conflicting strands. On the one hand there was a preoccupation with the rural, the Fenlands, coastal conditions – areas seldom touched by the architect's pencil. On the other, there was an interest in the mixed programme, hybrid spaces, technological finesse and structural gymnastics. Martyn Wiltshire's work as a member of Peter Wilson's unit during the 1984–5 academic year was a milestone in an aesthetic that combines the two and might be called 'techno-rustic'.

The unit worked on a series of proposals for the grounds of Clandeboye, an Irish stately home owned by the Marchioness of Dufferin and Ava. The propositions centred around three notions: new public uses, the house and stables, and the

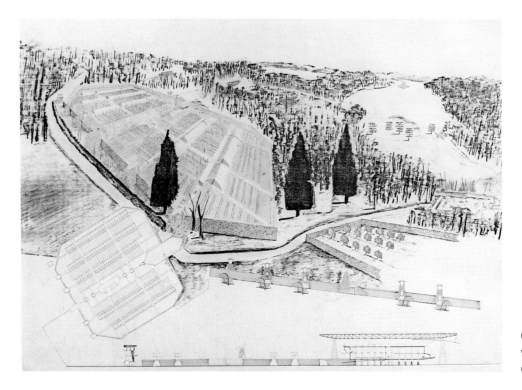

Clandeboye, 1984–5. Aerial view of walled garden with dining shed.

Techno-rusticity
Martyn Wiltshire

Clandeboye, 1984–5. Dining shed for artists and gardeners. Composite drawing.

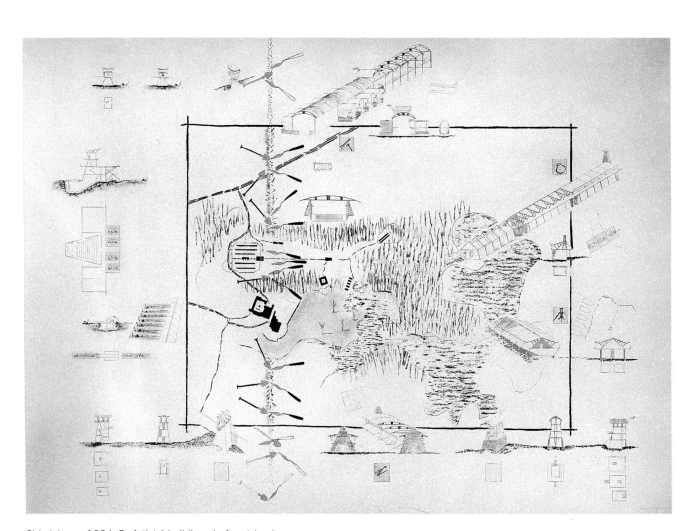

Clandeboye, 1984–5. Artists' buildings in forest landscape.

Clandeboye Institute. Peter Wilson wrote in the introduction to the 'Clandeboye Report':

> The projects illustrate the invention, confidence and constructive empiricism characteristic of the unit's efforts over the past several years. Avoiding the trap of neo-vernacular pastiche, the proposals respond poetically to the soft Irish landscape, employing such local materials as stone, wood and stucco. The spectrum of programmatic suggestions is overlaid by a gentle manifesto towards an architecture which possesses a descriptive and narrative dimension for the cultural enrichment of society as a whole.[1]

Wiltshire created a set of projects for the estate whose lyricism outstripped that of his contemporaries. One involved taking five existing farm buildings and determining a new mixed-use programme for city children: a motel/farm intended to educate children, through close proximity to animals, about the countryside and nature. As the 'Clandeboye Report' put it:

> The existing building pattern is interpreted and extrapolated as alternating strips of human and animal activity, maximising interaction and allowing for future expansion. The sequence of strips is tarmac, facilities, livestock, education, feathered, accommodation, and rare birds. Existing farm buildings are used as shells with independent insertions for new uses – dormitory, lectures, etc.[2]

The *Architectural Review* of August 1986 – the famed 'New Spirit' issue – explained the project thus:

> some distance from the privacy of the house [it] accepts the existing collection of five farm buildings, generating an overall strategy for linear expansion. The existing shells provide the sites for independent insertions, which take on new uses: a storage pit becomes a lecture

hall, and a family of barns becomes a dormitory. The insertion is figurative, using rural technology and iconography.[3]

For many, the images that have stayed in the mind's eye are those associated with a project for an Institute for Artists and Gardeners 'close to the main house and within a walled garden'. This was described by *AR* as follows:

> Evolving around a principal building, which straddles the garden wall, it has a shed-like quality, expressed by the large mechanical wing. Two giant rolling doors represent the characters of the gardeners and the artists respectively, involving them in the ritual of building. The canopy remains independent of the insertion – a dining shed.[4]

Here, Wiltshire comes alive with a stunning display of engineering specificity combined with the distinct organic patina of the rural. His sections have a simple elegance. They combine the eloquence of the traditional windmill and the echoey, tinniness of the cowshed. The building is highly ordered yet is not fussy. It has a sort of expediency that beguiles the viewer into aesthetic acceptance.

Compositionally, the drawings themselves are almost as hybrid as their proposition. There are structural sections, perspectival sections, landscape, site plan, narrative joinery, all juxtaposed with enough space around them for each representation to read coherently. These are austere spaces that have a kind of errant

Clandeboye, 1984–5. Dormitory building within existing galvanised iron shed.

20

purity; they depend on setting up an architectural rhythm then crossing it, either with the orthogonal and the diagonal, or using the A-A-A structural grid plus the sudden introduction of a rogue element.

Also included in *AR*'s 'New Spirit' issue was a facsimile of 'Across Architecture', a publication edited by Dimitri Vannas and Roland Cowan, two AA students. Their piece, called 'On a Kinetic Theory of Architecture', attempted to nail down work such as Wiltshire's:

> Everyday events are challenged by being given an extraordinary, unpredictable volume or location. All is the outcome of overlaying narrative onto a volume . . . The initial simplistic volume is progressively articulated, so that the material that defines it generates its own narrative, using the structural principle as an ordering device. Dimensional description is not appropriate here. Planes become articulated and begin to acquire character. Elements which interrupt the plane stressing the power of its solidity, becoming reference points for describing space and anticipating movement. Sequence is essential in these works.[5]

It is sequence that Wiltshire does so well: the choreography of space and time, material and programme – the essence of architecture.

Notes

1   Peter Wilson and Unit 1, 'Clandeboye Report', Architectural Association, 1985.

2   Ibid.

3   EM Farrelly (ed), 'The New Spirit', *Architectural Review*, August 1986.

4   Ibid.

5   Ibid.

Thematic discord

Peter Wilson and Architekturburo Bolles-Wilson

Peter Wilson is part of the star-studded coterie who taught at the Architectural Association, London, in the 1980s. Many of these bright lights were home grown, a self-referential gestation that was responsible for the great outpouring of talent at the AA during that time.

As a student, Wilson's first AA mentor was Dalibor Vesely, a major influence on a generation of AA-trained architects. After collaborating with Jeanne Sillett on a 1974 thesis project in Dorset, Wilson took a year to make his next significant move, his Water House of 1975. 'I don't think I really settled down until a year or two after I left the AA as a student – not until I did the Water House,' he has claimed. 'This is an architecture that refuses to become engaged. I had been

Water House, 1975.

22

through the political times of the late 1960s and somehow didn't feel at one with the ideology of dissent. I retreated and tried to find a degree zero.'[1]

Recently, Wilson has written of the project:

> this withdrawn and profoundly sensual design (Bachlard's *Poetics of Space*) attempted a simultaneous critical distance with a nevertheless precise formal prescription. The semantic ambitions of this contemporary 'architecture parlance' became very soon after blurred by the Jencksian Quagmire . . . The house is a mechanism, domesticating a mountain stream, the point of origin of a canal. In the four symmetrical corners of the house are four identical bathrooms – caldarium, sudatorium, frigidarium and tepidarium.[2]

The primal view of the world postulated in the Water House was further explored in a series of projects that included the Public Convenience of 1976. Wilson describes it as

> a somewhat over-didactic piece, again with the theme of utility and self-authenticating experience. The plan is symmetrical, two platforms approached via a central ramp. To the left, recognisable, culturally coded paired doors, washroom and cubicles. To the right, plan geometry mirrored, use denied. Earth – rock – water.

From the top: Water House, 1975; Public Convenience, 1976; Millbank Housing Competition, 1977.

In contrast to the soon-to-come 'Bridgebuilding and Shipshape' period of Wilson's career, projects like the Water House and the Public Convenience have an 'other-worldly' feeling – a brooding, quirky, surreal silence and impenetrability. They still draw on the Vesely-influenced rendering techniques of misty, steamy, crayoned shadow and sfumato colours and textures, yet they are also extremely formally explicit, with the architectural fundamentalism of the primitive hut or the monu-mental megalith.

The 1977 Millbank Competition employs a rationalist, yet almost Arcadian archi-tecture. It plays with the idea that the Thames will one day flood and transform its courtyards and gardens into formal lakes populated by a choreography of pavil-ions on flooded bases. The shadowy world continues, this time aided by the romantic yet murky depths of the foreboding Thames:

> Themes of water and ritual tried here on an urban and actual situation. Theoretical causality relativised by irregular circumstance. Between housing colonnade and street an overtly funereal garden and Italianate parking podium. I think I was reading De Sade's *120 Days of Sodom* at the time. Again the term 'postmodernism' had not been

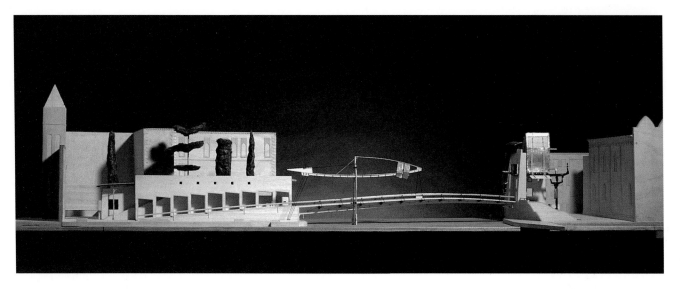

Accademia Bridge, Venice, 1982.

invented. We dropped many of the overtly referential themes here as soon as it was.

The watershed for Wilson took place some time at the beginning of the 1980s, when the figurative took hold and the ship shape and bridge invaded his work. These formal motifs were augmented by sculptural 'sticky-out-pieces', an interest in the Italian Memphis guys and a propensity to collage structural systems in each piece no matter what the scale. Historical reference all but disappeared in the schemes, or became more deeply embedded in its moves and strategies.

An iconic piece of this era was the 1982 Accademia Bridge, Venice, designed for the Biennale exhibition:

> A *filigrane*, finger-like vertebrae reaching from one side of the Grand Canal and, with the help of a rather dubious flying truss, just touching the Accademia bank. Arrival portico and pavilion supported by boat beam and figure. A discontinuity of components is here elevated to the level of a rather mannerist contextualism.

The Accademia Bridge was part of a catalogue of work including proposals for the Pont des Arts, Paris, 1982; Opera de la Bastille, 1983; Domplatz Housing, 1983; and the Clandeboye Project, 1984. The Clandeboye proposals were both a pedagogic brief for his AA unit and a chance for Wilson to hone his ideas in the specificity of the Irish stately landscape. (See pp16–21 for Martyn Wiltshire's work as part of that unit.) Wilson contributed a Gate House and two bridges to the project: an 'Endless Bridge' and the 'First Clandeboye Bridge'.

Peter Wilson and Architekturburo Bolles-Wilson

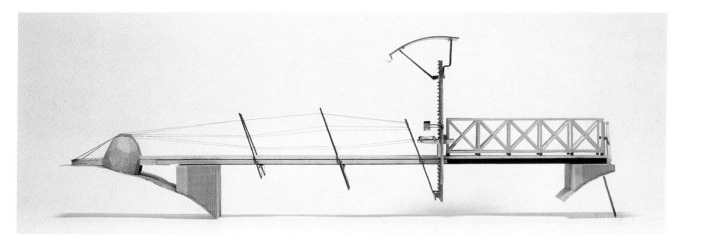

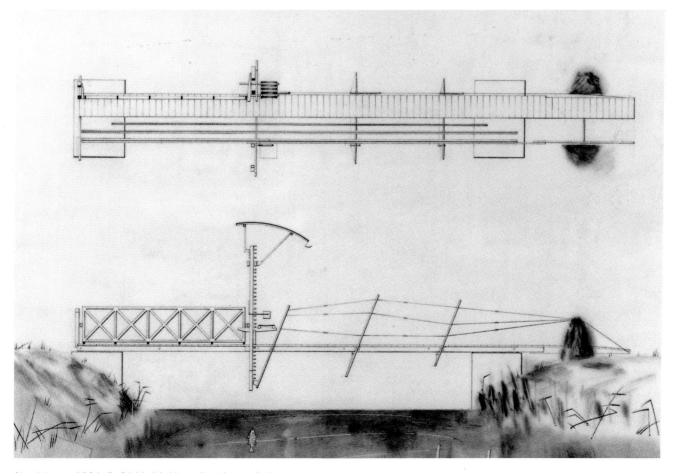

Clandeboye, 1984–5. Divided bridge: elevation and plan.

Clandeboye, 1984–5.
Divided bridge.

The bridge for us – perhaps because of Heidegger's wonderful
'Building, Dwelling, Thinking' – has long been an iconic convergence
of material and existential issues; the object that brings its location
into existence, the logical and sometimes purposefully less than
efficient collaboration of materials, and a moment of suspension
snatched from the continuity of everyday experience.

As the 1980s progressed into dusk, Wilson's work centred on Germany and Japan.
Many eloquent projects sought to expand further his formal and ideological lexicon.
Often, he tried to make explicit the differences between working in these separate
cultural fields. The 1988 'Forum of Sand' was one such attempt:

A pre-Potsdamer Platz voided centre (two years before the
reunification of the two Germanys). The exactitude of Mies and the
multiplicity of Scharoun are here played out as parallel themes. The
bridge is a found object with service adjacencies. In fact the same

The Forum of Sand,
Berlin, 1988.

bridge that Mies passed under daily as site architect for Beherens AEG Factory. The Mechanical Car Parks are transformations of the geometry of a Hapaq-Lloyd steamer, the Havel and Spree (Berlin's rivers). Crossing the sand circle is a pre-digital folded surface.

The breakthrough came with the Munster Library (1985), finally, a built project of some magnitude. This heralded a new transition in the work and a period of building that has lasted ten years. Long may it continue. Wilson's work of the 1980s continues to excite new generations of students and I sense that he has more fans that even he himself knows. We must leave the last word to him:

> I feel somewhat like a dinosaur digging out these old pieces. For us, they represent a very necessary and protracted prelude to our just over ten years of building. They were engaged on various levels with the discourses of the time; quite a different time from that of our current digital flights.

Notes

1   Peter Wilson, 'Bridgebuilding and Shipshape', *AA Publications Folio*, 1985.

2   Wilson, letter to the author, 17 May 2000. All subsequent quotations are from this source.

Appliance landscapes

Carlos Villanueva Brandt

Like Mark Prizeman and Neil Porter, Carlos Villanueva Brandt was a student of Nigel Coates in the pre NATØ days of the 1981–2 academic year at London's Architectural Association. Also like Prizeman and Porter, he was asked to make a proposal for the 'Giant-Sized Baby Town' project. His drawn proposal, whilst still utilising the fashionable 'sketched' aesthetic of the time, utilised formal one-point perspectives and ruled set-up lines. Looking back, one can sense that the distinct and accurate placement of elements was already a concern for him. Here, he describes his proposition, 'The Timber Fibre Factory':

> The fragment of the Isle of Dogs forming the site can be divided into four sections. The *tower*, inhabited by stacks of drying timber, stands

The Timber Fibre Factory, Isle of Dogs, 1981–2. Section.

28

The Timber Fibre Factory, Isle of Dogs, 1981–2.

upright at the entrance to this part of the island. Heating, burning and stacking, mingled with the fumes and sulphur, create a centre of activity. Transparent *wall houses* face the tower and join the fabric and motorbike factories in the chaos of the Lorry Park. *Venice,* a tightly designed structure, similar to a multi-storey car park, encourages active dialogue between different life styles. The *shed*, which protects the finished timber products, houses an enormous fireplace and canteen and is a stable fixture in the city. From it, activity radiates, as the timber panels shift from the shed to innumerable destinations. The industrial piazza sets up a dialogue between the two factory lines, referring both to the dock and the street.

Later in 1985, the heyday of NATØ, Brian Hatton described Villanueva Brandt's contribution to NATØ's 'Gamma City' exhibition at the Air Gallery in London:

The Timber Fibre
Factory. Tower.

> From [Prizeman's] *Dog* console one looked through Carlos Villanueva's 'Weirwall', a translucent screen of heat-buckled Perspex on charred posts, to his 'totem', a VDU, guts exposed and on the blink, atop a charred sleeper, with sacks of turnips strewn about. This bay was a sales pitch from an underviaduct industrial flea market with databased quotations, called TARMAC, and it was lit by a cantilevered neon lamp like an insect sprung from a slab of concrete . . .[1]

Here, we can still see some of Villanueva Brandt's earlier preoccupations: burning, charring and the nobility of detritus.

This, then, sets the scene for the close of the 1980s and the dawn of a new decade. Swiftly, Villanueva Brandt generated a couple of projects, in part eschewing the buckled detrital aesthetic, but evoking echoes of the NATØ landscape of technological redundancy and reuse. The first of these was an audacious scheme for the 1989 Mitsui Residential Design Competition, Japan, in which he came second. Toyo Ito, one of the judges, stated:

> I was most strongly interested in the second place winner by Brandt. More than architecture, it sets out to create scenery. Its map-like plan composition employs as code items such as rivers, linear walls, groves of posts, thin membrane covers, and scattered equipment. The way it proposes using characteristics of wood-structures – relation to the natural environment, openness, temporary nature, and so on – in totally new spaces, is extremely refreshing and impressive.[2]

Appliance landscapes
Carlos Villanueva Brandt

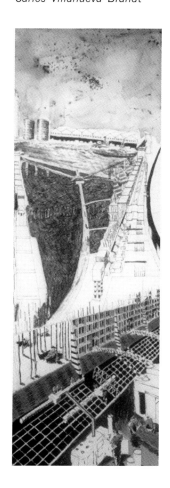

Above: The Timber Fibre
Factory, 1981–2.
Right: Downtown meets the
5 Continents, Yokohama, 1990.

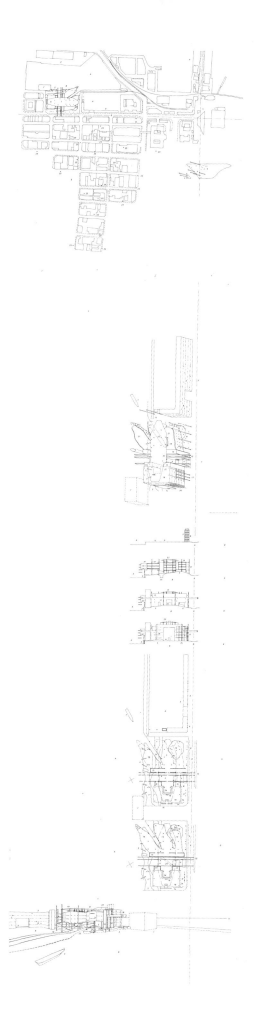

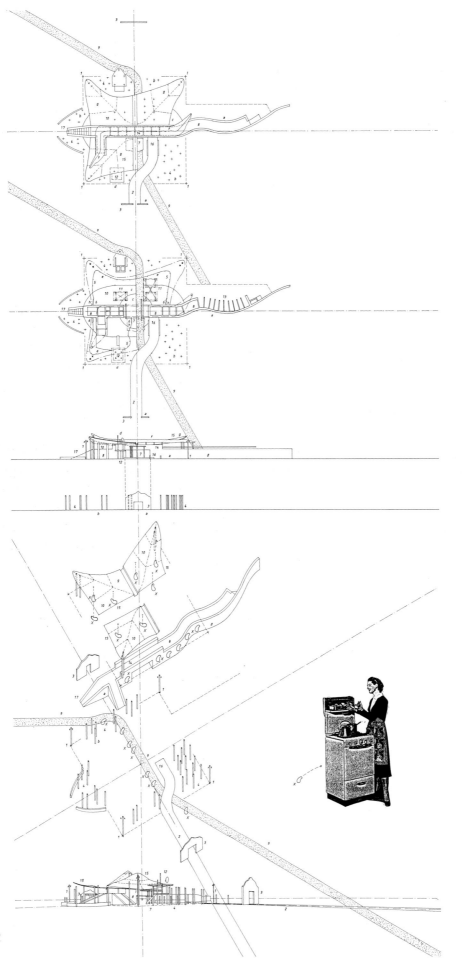

Indoor Landscape, 1989.

The scheme uses timber elements to create an 'In-door Landscape', which was then inhabited by domestic appliances. Domestic space is governed by the inter-action between appliance and user. There are three types of space housing domestic appliances, The Wall of Appliances, The River of Appliances and The Suspended Grid of Appliances.

The second project, which took some of these core ideas and expanded their lexicon, was called 'Downtown Meets the 5 Continents, Yokohama' (1990) and again configures a landscape of appliances, this time as part of a large series of 'Urban Components'. These included 21 audio/visual cameras, placed on the Downtown streets and transmitting live to The Park, which was made up of a series of loudspeakers attached to posts or concealed underground, and The Wall, which had 21 TV monitors, contained within an 8-metre-wide glazed office wall dividing Downtown from the port Kaigan Dori. Five sets of steps and moorings in the port symbolise the five continents. An artificial contoured landscape was positioned between the promenade and the waterfront. Again, the drawn, map-like notation was used to describe in enigmatic terms this new synthetic and cross-referenced landscape of shifting spaces.

Villanueva Brandt has attempted, with these two projects, to develop and rearticulate some of NATØ's strategic and formal language. This has resulted in a specific lexicon, which attempts to employ the fluctuating relationship between user and abuser, shine and rust and the consumer and the consumed. These important projects anticipate a variety of concerns and aesthetics that preoccupy many today and, I'm sure, will permeate architectural discussion for a number of years to come.

Notes

1   Brian Hatton, 'Produkti for Metamorpolis', *Architectural Association Files*, no 12, Summer 1986.

2   Competition Assessors Report, Mitsui House, International Design Competition, 1989.

Maverick deviations

Neil Spiller

I like architecture mythic, enigmatic, oblique and encrusted with decoration. I like it to suggest worlds, essences and supernatures. I despise the white, the simple and the tediously functional. I cannot bear the self-righteous minimalist or the cynical postmodern ironicist. My preferred historical architectural styles are the Baroque, Art Nouveau and the Gothic. (I was brought up in Canterbury, went to a school named after Geoffrey Chaucer, own a black cat with a musical taste that leans to the heavier side of rock – of course I have a sympathy for the Gothic.)

Spiller Farmer Architects. 'Turner House', Norfolk, 1990.

34

These are styles and aspirations that seek to imbue architecture with the organic, the natural and the vital. They have a wayward naughtiness that is never fully under control. But the thematic possibilities of the Gothic, with its menagerie of saints and sinners, priest and thieves, are almost infinite. The history of art is peppered with its motivating force from the Crucifixions of Dalí and Velázquez to Bacon's screaming popes and the ripped out genitals of the Chapman Brothers.

I started to study architecture in the late 1970s, a low point in architectural optimism. Thatcher's grip was tightening around our throats and the Yuppie was being created from the primordial filth. Neo-vernacular stalked the English sensibility and carbuncles were about to erupt on the faces of old friends.

My work of these fifteen years always sought to push the envelope of architectural discourse, creating new spaces where architecture might dwell. This quest first started with a reassessment of architectural ornament and narrative. A sound body of intellectual points of departure has always, for me, had to accompany projects. I value very highly the work of others that does not pander to current fashion and does not seek to be either popular or trendy. Successful work in my opinion always has a bit missed out; one might describe this quality as 'enigma'. A good piece of architecture should leave numerous 'handles' for the user, viewer and critic to grasp hold of and position it relative to a variety of arenas.

My search has taken me through all manner of terrain, from the design of a new architectural school for the Architectural Association – seeing the way architects are educated as a microcosm for society – via the issue of the representational column with its millennia of histories; large city master plans about time and its impact on the city; the mystical and cyclical process of alchemy; the virtual topologies of cyberspace, to the magic power of nanotechnology.

Fifteen years ago, sites were real and unassailable, architecture was simple and the architect's skills were less numerous. Architecture and architects looked relatively safe. One had only a few clues as to how the onslaught of technology would blow the doors off architecture's mini-minor. I started experimenting with an encrusted architecture, a series of filters, an architecture beyond the starkness of functionalism, an architecture whose way of representing itself was a combination of extravagant prose and a graphic gambit that was as powerful as it was invigorated, energetic and loose limbed. It owed very little to the established protocols of the prevailing Modernism. It was scary, it was sick, it was depraved and it was spiky. It played with wilful decadence and it took no prisoners and respected little. Its parents were a drunken Gothic and a sick anatomist's plaything crucified on an operating table. Indeed, an early work was described as a cockroach standing on its hind legs holding a spear.

In my work, reference to the Gothic has allowed me to create a body of work that faces the new millennium with an architecture that is optimistic, theatrical, interested in the grotesque, ornamental, schizophrenic, vitalist, mythic and highly strung. This does not imply that our future architectures will have the same set of clothes with which historical Gothic cloaks itself. Our pot-bellied gargoyles, pious saints and dusty echoes will be very different. Ours will be an architecture of ecological wefts, technological distortions and here and there digital necromancy. The spell is back, mixing together disparate things; spatial embroidery is where my architecture is going. It is a world populated by vacillating objects, Dalían exuberances, smooth but jagged objects and Baroque ecstasies. Objects will flit across a variety of spatial terrains simultaneously, some seen, some not. These ideas demolish the notion of the privileged site plan because the new objects in some sense become ubiquitous, doppelganged and paranoid.

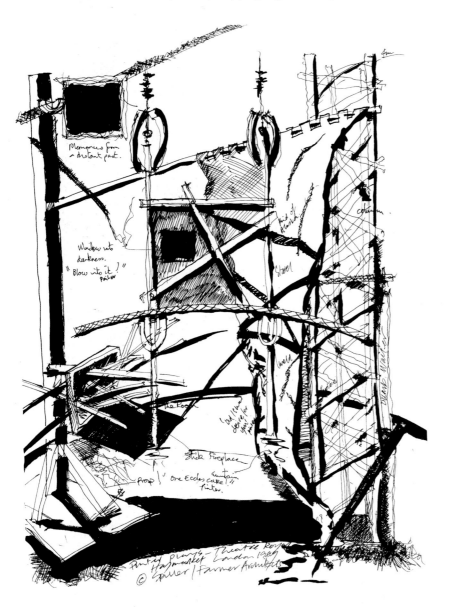

Left: Spiller Farmer Architects, Pinter plays sets, Theatre Royal, Haymarket, 1989. Below: Spiller Farmer Architects, Easels, Society of Architect Artists Exhibition, RIBA London, 1988.

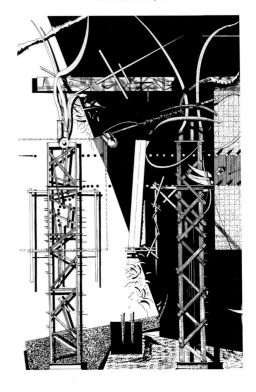

Maverick deviations
Neil Spiller

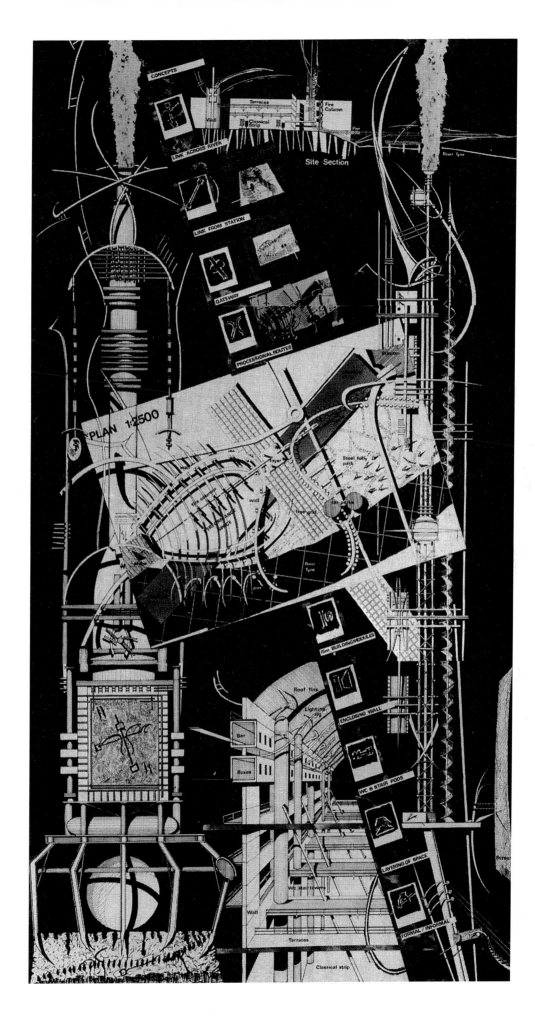

Spiller Farmer Architects,
Heavy Metal Cathedral,
Newcastle, 1989.

Samite semiotics

Kevin Rhowbotham

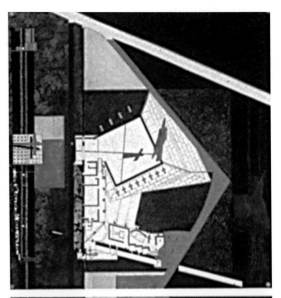

Out of all the work I enjoyed and was inspired by in the 1980s, Kevin Rhowbotham's Rosythe Church is out on its own. Rhowbotham is an architectural evangelist. Like all evangelists he often calls for the shedding of much that has become unquestioned, familiar and fully accepted. He exposes the sophist with clear, sharp, pointed polemic. His work is unsentimental, yet he himself has a sentimental streak that sometimes shows as a warm chink in his armour of correctness, burning righteousness and revolutionary zeal.

At the time of the Rosythe Church (1984) Rhowbotham wrote: 'The practice of architecture is progressively constrained by a weight of cant and misinformation . . . There is now an urgent need for conjecture, speculation and research . . . to strike at the heart of the subject',[1] and this is still true today.

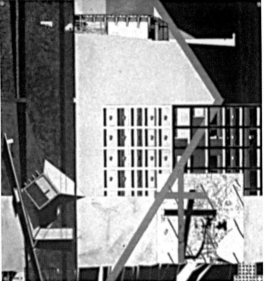

With the Rosythe Church proposal, architecture is indeed struck in its heart – a heart of semiotics, texture, enigma and sheer compositional dexterity. This entrancing project is on the cusp of rationalism, deconstruction and Cubist protocols, yet hints at Rhowbotham's future work of form versus programme and his urban masterplan field studies.

The church drawing is a long, tripartite one, a vertical triptych. The first thing that instantly grabs the viewer is its sheer graphic power. Its meanings and internal relationships become clear as one's eyes skirt over its beautifully wrought surface. As you link this with that, site plan with elevation and detail, you are still never quite sure which Rosythe Church you are admiring, or even whether you yourself have invented this particular version out of a collection of alternatives secreted throughout the drawings.

Rosythe Church, 1984, in association with Robin Sargeant, Janette Emery.

Samite semiotics
Kevin Rhowbotham

The sheer guts of this drawing dominated the '40 Under 40' exhibition, held in 1984, which attempted to define a moment in mid-1980s 'architectural youth'. Its knowing navigation of a variety of thematic and spatial preoccupations showed up many of the other exhibitors for the paucity of their ambition and talent. The drawing had the same effect in EM Farrelly's seminal 'New Spirit' issue of *Architectural Review* in August 1986.

What is perhaps less well known about Rhowbotham is that he passed through the offices of OM Ungers, another exponent of the well-articulated orthogonal plan and indeed a rampant Classical pastichist. What this proves about Rhowbotham is that here is someone in full control of architecture's semiological languages. The textural quality of the Rosythe drawing has a visceral intensity. Once seen, this drawing and building are tattooed into the memory.

Right: Rosythe Church 1984.
Below: Parliament Square Competition, 1984,
in association with Robin Sargeant, Fiona Daly, Janette Emery.

In the mid to late 1980s, Rhowbotham never missed an opportunity to push the art of architectural representation to its limit. In an era perhaps dominated by Stirling's worm's-eye axonometric, Rhowbotham's work was a refreshing antidote to which I could constantly return for inspiration and the comforting feeling that architecture could entail more than I'd been led to believe. It could certainly be more naughty and quirky.

The next time I saw a Rhowbotham drawing, it too seared itself into my memory. It was his competition entry for the Parliament Square Competition (1984), which,

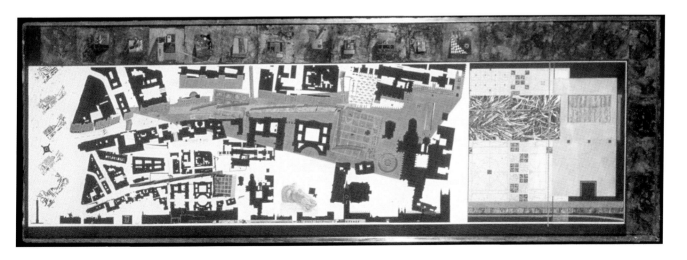

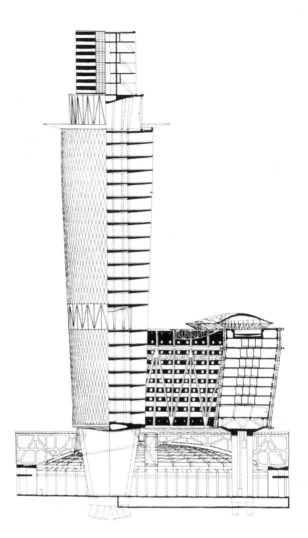

Project in association with
Robin Sargeant, Birmingham,
1985. Section.

incidentally, it won. The competition was simply to deal with the large grassed roundabout that is Parliament Square, opposite the Palace of Westminster in London. The site was at the heart of the UK's executive, surrounded by Parliament and Whitehall. Typically, he attempted to reconcile an area larger than the brief's site and included Whitehall almost up to Trafalgar Square. Nelson's Column can be seen in plan and elevation on the left of the drawing. Again, the piece is long but this time in landscape as opposed to the church's portrait. It is not instantly recognisable as from the same hand as that of the church, yet after a moment's thought, it is obvious. I would like to describe the drawing and scheme as 'samite' – a rich medieval dress fabric of silk occasionally interwoven with gold. The scheme is quasi-medieval with its jousting runways and heraldic motifs, reconstituted from Elizabeth I's time. Around the square is a zone of monuments to British heroes and an art wall exhibiting some of the nations indigenous artworks. Compositionally, the project is about various degrees of enclosure that redefine pedestrian circulation to enhance what is, or should be, important. The tactic of representing different views on the same drawing and rejoicing in their coincident juxtaposition is maintained,

Samite semiotics
Kevin Rhowbotham

Birmingham, 1985.

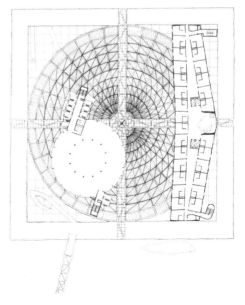

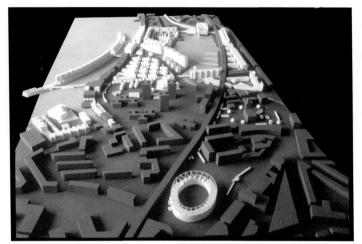 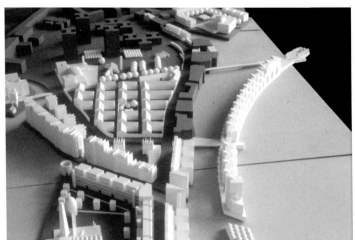

Limehouse, 1986–7; project in association with South Bank Polytechnic Diploma students.

Samite semiotics
Kevin Rhowbotham

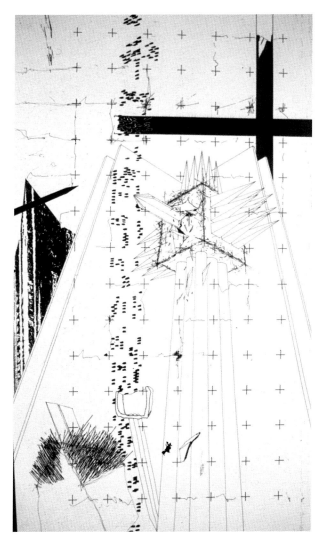

Conceptual sketch.

augmented here by a series of painterly vignettes of some of the scheme's set pieces and a close-up of the artwall. Interestingly, the *Horse of Selene* appears on the drawing. What a strange clue Rhowbotham leaves for us to attempt to decode his intentions! Selene is the mythic characterisation of the moon. What is Rhowbotham signalling to us? That the British Empire and its imperial significance will further wane, or that this work is a collage of time as well as a collage of architectural elements? Or is this a '*Godfather*' horse's head, a gift to that which is about to die? Or am I barking up the wrong tree? Whatever the intended meaning of the horse's head, this is another classic of lost architecture.

In recent years, Rhowbotham developed ideas of Non-Specific-Urbanism (NSU), co-founded FAT, evolved considerable dexterity on computers, and published the books *Form to Programme* (1995) and *Field Event/Field Space* (1999). He is an inspirational teacher. I, for one, look forward to the next tranche of Rhowbotian invective, sublime architectures and polemical prose. It is good to see him back in good old Blighty again after various foreign visiting professorships. Few produce immortal work. Rhowbotham is one of them. He may agitate, unbalance and frighten, but we need characters like Kevin Rhowbotham.

Notes

1   Kevin Rhowbotham, Rosythe Church, EM Farrelly (ed), 'The New Spirit', *Architectural Review*, August 1986.

Argon cutting in the industrial wilderness

Mark Prizeman

Like Neil Porter and Carlos Villenueva Brandt, Mark Prizeman was a student of Nigel Coates at the Architectural Association from 1981–2. Also like Porter, he was called upon to make a proposition for the 'Giant-sized Baby Town' on London's Isle of Dogs. The following is part of his poetic description of his aims and notions for this project. His narrative betrays a characteristic nostalgia for the technologically defunct, finding sublimity in the mechanised systems and the neon-soaked dance of the contemporary city:

> What would life be without the *Jungle* the animal power of the smokestack? An umbilical cord pumps liquid sulphur to a heavy chemical works, by the still dockside, from the heavy dispatch jetty. Weaving its way across the Dog's Isle, subsidiary industries cluster, houses breed and work is forgotten. Between the conurbations, where the pylons stride, lie the Saharas of wilderness punctuated by the odd café or pink rubber cone. Taking a walk across these wastes one views the hives of activity as a warren for the creative senses. For work here is not treated as a means to an endless supply of Cortinas or Sandy Shaw records but as a trigger to enable minds to fester.

> Traversing the pharmaceutical factory is a large canteen. Industrial cooking facilities are provided, prams pass dinner parties, the factory hooter sounds, donating a note to a moment in time to start work or to go to bed. The workers by the magazine stall, trying to stay awake on dawn raids, pick their noses and gaze at the aircraft-dismantling yard across the road. Lorries swoosh past in the drizzle, the argon cutter faintly illuminates the storage tanks casting long shadows on the depot hotels, someone changes a record over and a few notes change hands.

> Lying on your back, the sodium orange lights rest in stripes across a Persian carpet. Looking out of the window, the waste pipes burst like

Argon cutting in the industrial wilderness
Mark Prizeman

Right and below: Giant-sized
Baby Town, Chemical Works,
1982.
Bottom: Under Vulcan's wing.
Vignette.

an exhaust driving you towards the intoxication of distant highly illuminated towers, chimneys and ramps.[1]

Prizeman's interest in redundancy and the rejuvenation of obsolete technology found another outlet in the 1989 proposal for the resurrection of a Vulcan bomber within a commercial building. According to Prizeman, 'The actual plane had been bought at auction in 1989 by Robert Lance-Hughes, a former officer in the Royal Engineers who had turned his hand to property development'. The project became 'lost' because of 'the apocryphal property recession about this time ... I suspect the plane was sold for scrap as the price of those metals soared in the mid-90s'.[2]

The notion of taking expensive industrial hardware, with its normally short life span and then occupying its spaces as part of a larger concept is an interesting proposition. One can think of many examples where such an approach would have created interesting, original spaces, that, whilst having a sense of industrial history, might contribute to new ways of urban and rural living. Such a notion could produce the antithesis of the normal strip-out-and-paint-white architectural approach to redundant industrial buildings.

Ground floor and gallery
vignettes.

After the Vulcan, Prizeman embarked on a series of projects that investigated aircraft construction and lightweights, an example of which is his 'Austen Door', made like an aircraft wing. Prizeman lost this project in the sense that he 'spent hours and hours and hours making it and haven't dared check whether it is still standing in Royal Hospital Road'.[3]

Earlier in his career, Prizeman was a member of the avant-garde group NATØ (Narrative Architecture Today), fronted by Nigel Coates. His debris-chic projects of this period were instantly recognisable. His product and graphic work were an integral part of any NATØ show. An example of this is his contribution to the 1985 exhibition 'Gamma City' at the Air Gallery in London, described by Brian Hatton as follows:

> At the end of the zebra crossing stood an old BSA motorcycle/sidecar, filled with onions, and beside it a tangled console of welded junk. This was the DJ playdeck from *Radio Dog,* a film starring Mark Prizeman, author of these *produkti*. Opposite was another assemblage of cannibalised durables by Prizeman, the entrance to his

Argon cutting in the industrial wilderness
Mark Prizeman

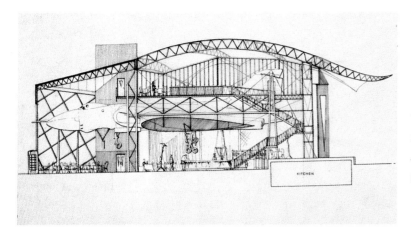

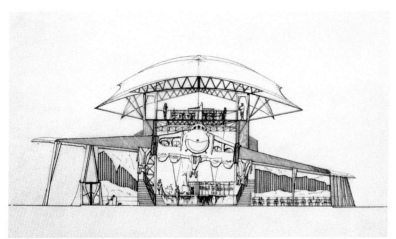

'Gunfetish Club' a fictional institution from *Radio Dog*.[4]

It seems that this affinity for the technologically redundant and its innate sculptural possibilities continues to inspire Prizeman's work. As technology becomes so smart it all but disappears, what can we do with its historical, visible residue but reuse it for Baroque sculpture and outlaw events?

Notes

1   Mark Prizeman, 'The Discourse of Events', *Themes 3*, Architectural Association, 1983.

2   Mark Prizeman, letter to author, 2000.

3   Ibid.

4   Brian Hatton, 'Produkti for Metamorpolis', *Architectural Association Files*, no 12, Summer 1986.

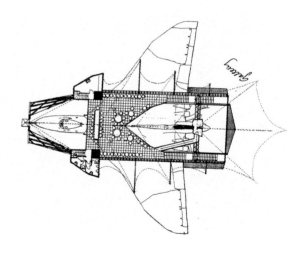

Vulcan Building. Left, from the top: sections and exterior perspective; above: plan.

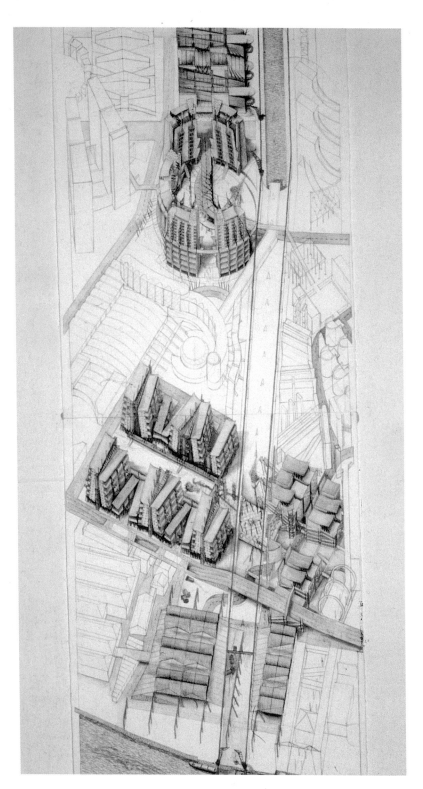

Giant Sized Baby Town 1981–2. Axonometric.

Architectural kinematics

Neil Porter

In 1981, Neil Porter was a student of Nigel Coates at the Architectural Association in London. This academic year, the unit's preoccupations revolved around the dysfunctional docklands area of the Isle of Dogs, at the time a fitting name for this part of London. The 'Dogs' was an area of industrial degradation and neglect; the sinister, massive water bodies of the docks themselves were rarely used. This was the landscape of various episodes of *The Sweeney* and of John MacKenzie's 1979 film *The Long Good Friday*. They were run-down communities, imprisoned in the rough end of postwar Modernism and poor infrastructure, invisible to the rest of London. Coates' brief was based on the premise that

> the division of housing from industry
> results in the extraordinary blandness
> familiar along every step through to
> Milton Keynes . . . The year began
> with a project for a radio station,
> then . . .a video programme based
> on mixing the themes of home and
> work and on to a mesh of
> interlocked factory projects that
> spread over the whole of the island.
> 'Giant Sized Baby Town', as we
> called it, seemed the ideal way of
> unmasking a spirited kind of
> architecture built upon the wastes
> of urban decay.[1]

Above and right: Giant Sized Baby Town, 1981–2.

The dizzying NATØ projects were still a few years away (the group started up the following year), yet their preoccupations were already evolving. Porter experimented with a looser, sketchier drawing style that was seen to be appropriate within the unit but was still accurate and articulate. The task was to respond to this mixed-use functionality and industrial dynamic. Here, architecture and design needed to rejoice in the maelstrom of urban metamorphosis, decay and expediency. In Porter's hands, this does not result in urban nihilism but creates a new set of visual, social and dynamic aesthetics. Its codes and artful processes are at first shocking but once learnt become oddly evocative and romantic. Porter describes his 'Furniture Precinct' project in the following terms:

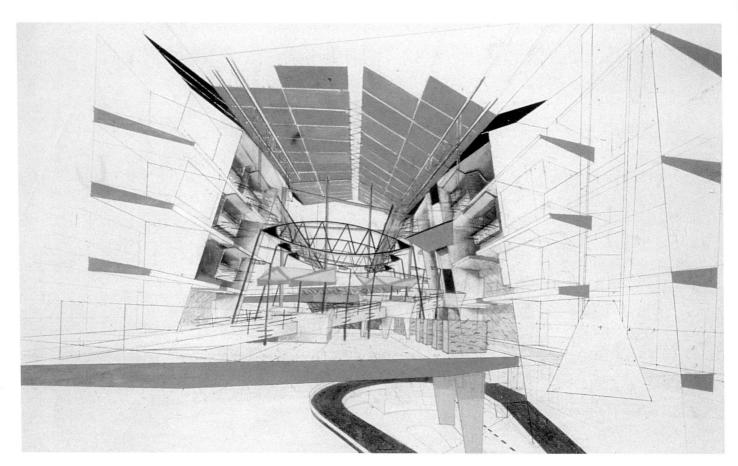

BBC Headquarters, London.
Control room.

Perched on the precipice of his balcony, the householder scans the work processes below. Splicing through the scene, the track of the gantry crane links his particular view to the sequential activities which compose the territory of the furniture of the factory: an elongated form stretching right from the river to the dock.

In fact the process begins as the crane picks up raw material from a vast hypermarket, to carry it northwards towards the Processing Square; the place that combines public meeting with momentary glimpses of products in transit. Here materials are distributed to work halls within which a new breed of artisans live and work. They bring their materials into their living rooms – rooms that tilt inwards towards the work halls, as if held by the machines. The various parts of furniture that emerge are passed on to an assembly plant up by Millwall Dock. This plant provides a rallying point for the whole island by doubling up as a nightclub.[2]

Leaving the politics of this project aside (to me they seem to differ little from the Thatcher dream of the time, suggesting a hedonistic, ludic, grease-monkey population), its real strength is Porter's correlation between the vectors of industrial

50

Architectural kinematics
Neil Porter

Hypermarket Calais.
Above: site plan;
right: shelving.

production and the spectacular spaces and opportunities that can be developed in their interstices. His interest in the typology of the hypermarket was continued with a hypermarket in Calais and a project for the BBC developed after he defected to Peter Wilson's AA unit for the 1982–3 season.

These projects laid the groundwork for the mature Porter, illustrating an evolving graphic style that is becoming more direct, better rendered and more strategic in its micro conditions. This maturity is best exemplified by his entry for the 1987 competition to celebrate the bicentenary of the French Revolution. Here, Porter describes the work's intentions:

> *Parade*, the famous Diaghilev-Cocteau ballet, is taken as a narrative overlay for the Place de la Bastille. An onstage choreography of festival buildings is placed on traffic islands surrounding the Colonne de Juillet. They are juxtaposed against off-stage noises, arising from the Bassin de l'Arsenal, a pleasure port already under development.
>
> An 'acrobat, conjurer, and American girl' supply the buildings with character and event. Acting as a focal point they attract an audience, and then send it off in the direction of the 'managers'. A series of

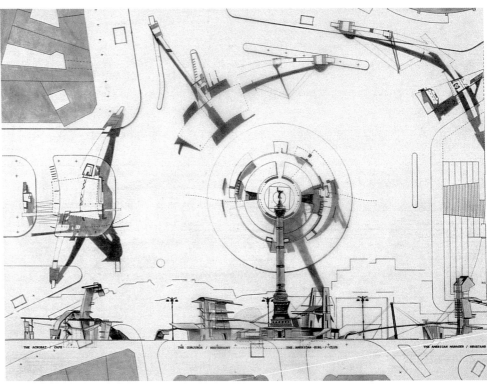

Above and right: Parade, Place
de la Bastille, Paris, 1987–9.

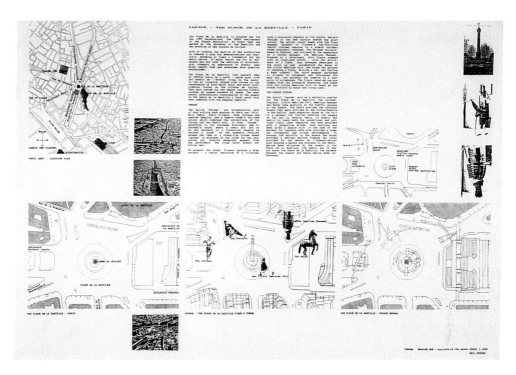

Parade, Place de la Bastille, Paris, 1987–9.

towers that supports a seesaw auditorium also acts as an entrance to the Bassin. The resultant parade-ground is placed to celebrate the enthusiasm of the populace of Paris; a spontaneous flash–point for the city's demonstrations and festivities.[3]

Here, Porter shows a poetic understanding of the changing dynamic of urban, theatrical and social celebratory space. The project is a cocktail of delicately poised structures perched around the Place, and the installations, their views and cuts are carefully considered. The individual buildings are composed to stress the near independence of each functional element. Each floor, balcony, stairway and roof is artfully conjoined. But fundamentally, Porter shows us that he understands the movement at special times in this part of Paris and creates an architecture that seeks never to interrupt these vectors. His tactics – the exploitation of an episodic choreography of space – are also those of the landscape architect, and it is not surprising that he is now the London partner of landscape architect Kathryn Gustafson.

Notes

1   Nigel Coates, 'The Discourse of Events', *Themes 3*, Architectural Association, 1983.

2   Neil Porter, ibid.

3   EM Farrelly (ed), 'The New Spirit', *Architectural Review*, August 1986.

Vaults of imagination

Ben Nicholson

Ben Nicholson's work is admired by many. It has a resonance that seems to cut across the aesthetic and philosophical entrenchments of the architectural cognoscenti. The projects have something to say about the everyday (the Divine in the mundane), satisfy the form-throwing pyrotechnic constituency, but also attempt a continuity with the historical basis of architecture, its symbolism, proportion and ritual. Nicholson, above all, is a powerful architect whose genius is intensely personal, idiosyncratic yet not esoteric. He has developed a style that is particular, premeditated and learned.

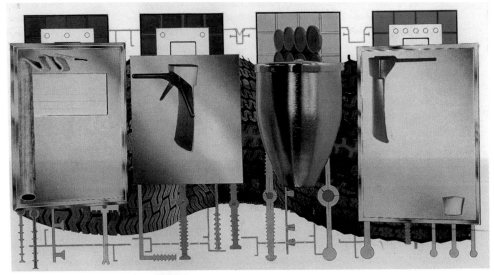

Appliance House, 1987.
Interior studies.

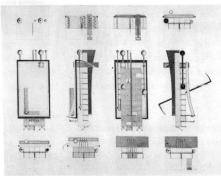

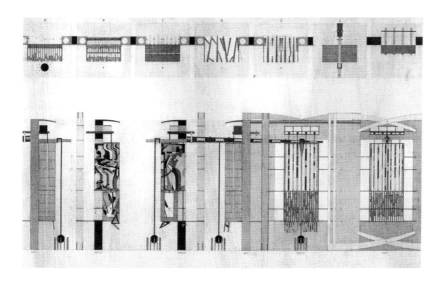

Appliance House, 1987.
Elemental studies.

Nicholson is best known for his Appliance House (1987). Here, he explains its thematic preoccupations:

> At the outset, three themes were developing simultaneously. One was the desire to coerce the discipline of painting into the discipline of architecture; another was to bring into focus the pragmatic quality of *Sweets*([a catalogue] for America's construction industry) with the frivolity of the *Sears* catalogue (for America's consumers). The third theme I was working on was studying the reciprocities between Michelangelo's Sistine ceiling frescoes and the architecture of the Laurentian Library. I was led to the rapport between these two masterworks because of a chance occurrence while I was setting up slide projectors before giving a talk about the two works. Because slides of the Laurentian plan and the Sistine ceiling are long and skinny they would not fit easily on the screen; one of the two projectors was then accidentally moved, causing the two slides to lie on top of each other.[1]

The projects that preceded the seminal Appliance House are rarely published. The first, 'Travulgar Square' (1978), was conceived when Nicholson was a student at London's Architectural Association. This project is possibly the weirdest featured in this book. Its biological formalism harbours Nicholson's wide-ranging aspirations for architecture. It exhibits a willingness to engage in politics, urban design, mixed

Travulgar Square Scheme

Let us presume the city responds through its buildings to the needs and ideals of its culture at any given time. As example is Trafalgar Square as it was conceived in the 19th C. Britain was supreme on the Battlefield (Nelson's Column), had a Culture (National Gallery), had an Empire (Canada and South Africa House), a Monarchy (Admiralty Arch), a Government (Whitehall View) and Divine Guidance (St Martin's Church). In this scheme I propose to continue this translation of city mood into built form. This time, however, it is not the image of Imperialism but that of late Bourgeois Consumer Culture.

A trilogy of buildings is placed in the middle of Trafalgar Square. The street furniture is removed and the Square is graded and paved right up to the un-distrubed existing buildings. The three buildings emphasise different aspects of urbanity. The Palandromic Man describes Degradation and Beauty within our bodies, the Consumption Bird shows the ability of our culture to extract without giving anything in return, and lastly the Hands describe Hope for the future derived from the undestroyable past.

The existing streets leading from the corners of genteel London come physically and symbolically to dead ends evoking the crisis and its dissolution.

The Palandromic Man

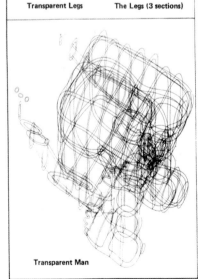

Transparent Legs   The Legs (3 sections)

Transparent Man

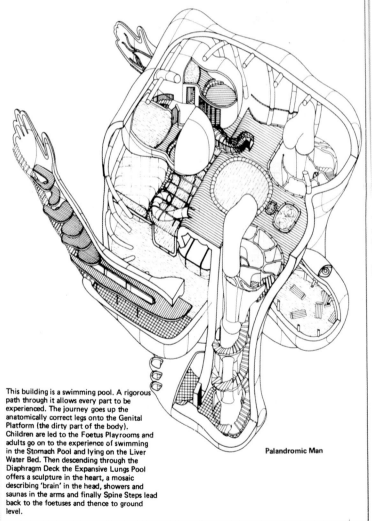

This building is a swimming pool. A rigorous path through it allows every part to be experienced. The journey goes up the anatomically correct legs onto the Genital Platform (the dirty part of the body). Children are led to the Foetus Playrooms and adults go on to the experience of swimming in the Stomach Pool and lying on the Liver Water Bed. Then descending through the Diaphragm Deck the Expansive Lungs Pool offers a sculpture in the heart, a mosaic describing 'brain' in the head, showers and saunas in the arms and finally Spine Steps lead back to the foetuses and thence to ground level.

Palandromic Man

uses, analogy, historical precedent and symbolism. Nicholson's work, even as a student, has an assured quality that is confident enough to experiment, combined with playful enthusiasm. He describes the basic premise of the scheme thus:

> let us presume the city responds through its buildings to the needs and ideals of its culture at any given time. An example is Trafalgar Square as it was conceived in the nineteenth century. Britain was supreme on the Battlefield (Nelson's Column), had a culture (National Gallery), had an Empire (Canada and South Africa House), a Monarchy (Admiralty Arch) and Divine Guidance (St Martin's Church). In this scheme I propose to continue this translation of city mood into built form. This time, however, it is not the image of Imperialism but that of late Bourgeois Consumer Culture. A trilogy of buildings is placed in the middle of Trafalgar Square. The street furniture is removed and the Square is graded and paved right up to the undisturbed existing buildings. The three buildings emphasise different aspects of urbanity. The Palindromic Man describes Degradation and Beauty within our bodies, the Consumption Bird shows the ability of our culture to extract without giving anything in return, and lastly the Hands describe hope for the future derived from the undestroyable past.[2]

The Palindromic Man is a swimming pool, supported on 'anatomically correct' legs, arms out to the sides and spaces within called the Foetus Playrooms and the Stomach Pool. Users later relax on a Liver Water Bed. The turn of the 1960s Bowellism of Webb and Outram takes extreme form and loses its non-committal form; here it is declared and surreal.

One can imagine that intellectual gymnastics such as these led Nicholson into Libeskind's Cranbrook Academy, a very small school devoted to exploring what architecture is and should be, unlike most architecture schools, which are symphonies of compromise, wary of the disapproving glance of those who practice mediocrity. Here, Nicholson developed the Grunewald House (1980), and his career has since become synonymous with house designs. This continuing study of the house as a microcosm for architecture and urbanity has created many marvellous, surreal and poetic vignettes of domestic life against a backdrop of architecture's incredibly virulent history. Each of the house projects is simultaneously a lens and a vessel through and in which to examine and contain ideas. Nicholson's world is undeniably modern yet rooted in history, audacity and knowledge, the result of long hours of study.

Opposite: Travulgar Square, 1979. Below: Grunewald House, 1980. Models.

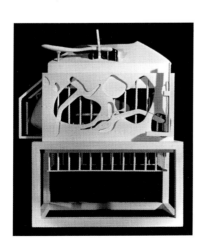

57

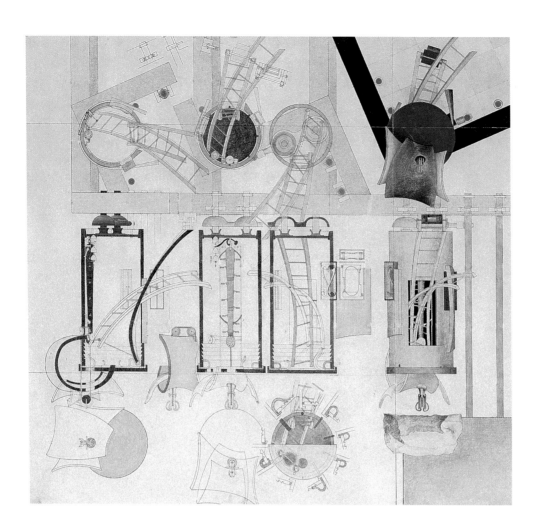

Above, right and opposite:
Grunewald House, 1980.
Elemental studies.

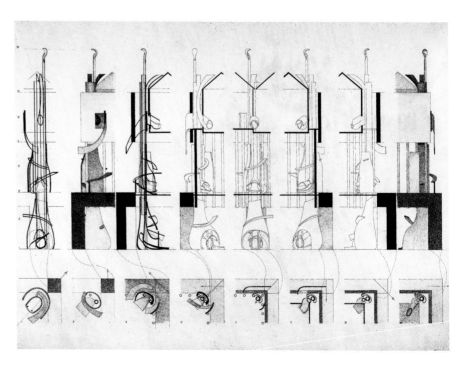

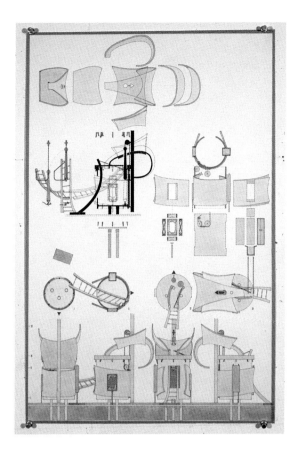

The Grunewald House is conceived as a vessel in tune with the Albertian conception of a house:

> The Grunewald House is composed of places identifiable with us. The fireplace remains, the bathing room, sleeping room and excreting room remain, cupboards are remembered, a balcony returns, an observation and fleeing post arrives, a room of contemplation arrives, the walls, floor, and roof remain. The house therefore stays as it always was, but this time it is returned in a manner comprehensible to modern man.[3]

The Grunewald House shows Nicholson to be a master draughtsman. Nothing in his work is randomly composed; the placement of shape relative to paper, of form relative to other forms and form relative to narrative is compulsively explored, tweaked and exploited. The Grunewald House has many grandfathers:

> The Drawings shown here are made for a House that is to embody the emotive and immeasurable requirements of man. By seriously addressing thinkers such as Freud, Heidegger, Baudelaire, Poe, Magritte, Munch and Bachelard, it is possible to form a house that no longer responds to long-worn and debatable notions, but rather is a response to an urban world teetering on the brink.[4]

One can only give a few short glimpses of this project; there is much more to learn from it. I for one will be ravenously combing every line and form for bits to savour, bits that will nourish the weary traveller. For Nicholson's work is an oasis in what can often be a terribly dry terrain.

Notes

1   Interview with Alvin Boyarsky, in Robin Middleton (ed), *The Idea of the City*, AA Publications (London), 1985.

2   Ibid.

3   Text supplied by Ben Nicholson.

4   Ibid.

Exquisite precision

CJ Lim

There is always an astounding quality to everything CJ Lim does. With its precise calibration and vivid use of colour, his work is crystal clear. It is also consistently big: not for him the A1 drawing, his sketches are metres long, or painted on eight by four foot MDF. That Lim is a perfectionist is without doubt; one can see in his work the result of continual reassessment, redrawing, rearticulation, and, above all, exquisite precision. Like all architects, he presents drawings that consist of codes and abstractions. It is part of the design process to choose how the viewer will see even these codes and the parts of the design that one wishes to expose to critical scrutiny. The, as yet, not fully formed remains mute, opaque, hidden and merely outlined. All architects do this but few are a virtuoso of the cunningly contrived vignette, the notational morphology and the stray rotation.

Peter Cook has traced Lim's architectural genealogy back to the halcyon days of the Architectural Association during the 1980s:

> Coming from Kuala Lumpur, CJ Lim could, I suppose, have had the choice to study in Singapore, Perth, Melbourne or London. Fortunately, after he finished his schooling in Northern England, he entered the Architectural Association. The time was the early 1980s, and the situation such that the brilliant students of Archigram,

Exquisite precision

CJ Lim

Dalibor Vesely or Rem Koolhaas and Elia Zenghelis were in the ascendant and drawing of a precise and magical quality was the *lingua franca*. The rise of graphic technique during this period at the AA was paralleled by an increased attention to the dexterity, complexity and finesse of the delineated shapes, edges and juxtapositions suggested in the drawings. 'Formalism' is the descriptive word that comes to mind, but the essentially pejorative associations that we attach to this word automatically suppress the power and emancipation we felt in the face of the increasingly beautiful and inventive things that were suggested in these drawings. A follower of Vesely would surround most suggestions of form and position by a telling sfumato of shade, patina and suggestions of light. Mystery and innuendo, as well as the surreal, were necessary for the representation and discussion of a world reacting to the directness of Modernism and 'High-tech', which was happening in the same city at the same time. By contrast, the legacy of Koolhaas and Zenghelis was one of precision and extreme formal clarity moving from a shared inheritance of de Stijl on the one hand, to Suprematism on the other. The intrinsic combination of symbolic wit that is present in much of the Russian work of the 1920s appealed to the OMA architects.[1]

Opposite and below: CJ Lim, Mark Smout, Dominique Leutwyler, Rachel Calladine, Architecture Centre, Newcastle, 1995.

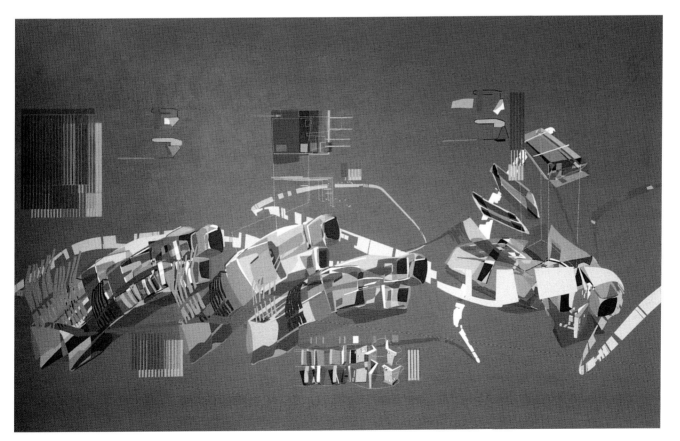

Terminal, Chicago. From the top: Aerial perspective; plan and sections.

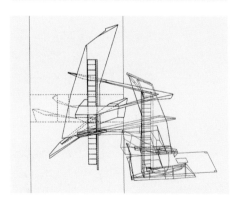

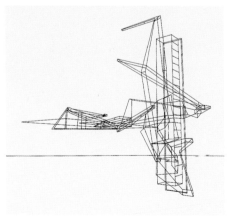

Lim's work is a catholic maelstrom of 'isms', simultaneously constructivist, deconstructivist, suprematist and Modernist. Yet this never becomes a mess. It is always delightfully restrained, even at its wildest. Lim has never been prone to the sort of crazy exuberance of some of his contemporaries; he is wily enough to claim a centre ground that is at once attractive, diligent and skilful. The disparate factions that exist in the academy, the profession and the press therefore value his work. Cook introduces his formal and compositional protocols:

> It was obvious that CJ Lim would be drawn towards [the Archigram] corner by a combination of inherited graphic skills and romanticism, and because he enjoyed designing rather than atmospherics, or the making of hard rhetorical statements. Again and again, . . . work that had a collective strength, challenging the rigidity of most plans and nearly all sections; challenging the pudding-like nature of substance, and the cloche-like nature of roofs; challenging the set piece nature of circulation and level by level crates of floors . . . However, the twisting sheets of glass and steel that characterised Lim's work at the time were unencumbered by social or cultural programmes. His buildings were essentially to do with skin and bones.[2]

Lim is a deft maker of skeletons and has an almost tailor-like appreciation of the cladding nip and tuck. This couture is steadfastly adhered to.

By the time of his AA thesis (1989), Lim's work already illustrated some of the longstanding preoccupations present in his work today. The project was for a 'Terminal for the Linear Car, Chicago'. Lim literally redefined the city by the simple tactic of reversing its ordering and entering protocols. He reoriented the entrance to city tower blocks to the top via his linear cable car.

More recently, Lim has been particularly successful in architectural competitions (those fine generators of projects lost for ever, often even if one wins). Two missed opportunities, however, are Clone House and Urban Metazoo (both 1999), the former described by Lim as follows:

> The house is centred on four identical and interchangeable chambers. There is no hierarchy to these units. The contents are a sleeping element, a computer workstation, and a glass overhead plane of uninterrupted sky. The four rooms may be hoisted up or stacked to reconfigure the space for different eventualities. The house can as a result accommodate up to five occupants, reflecting the changing spatial requirements as one progresses through life.[3]

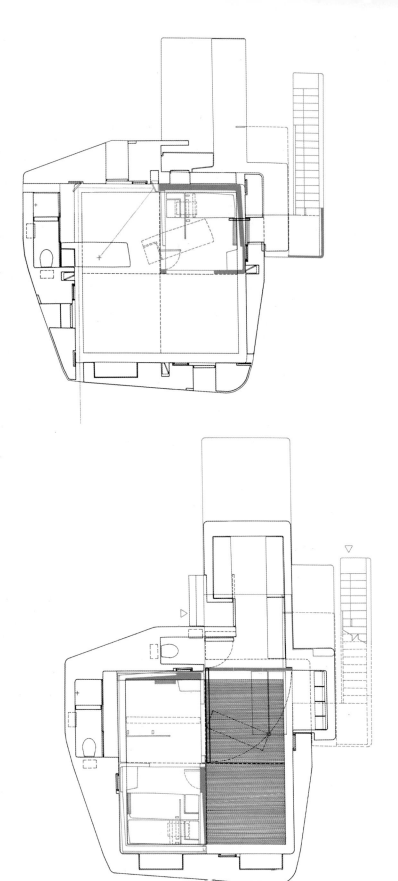

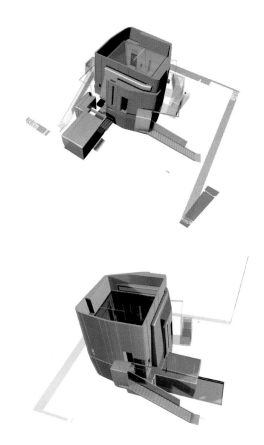

CJ Lim, Ed Lui, Hans Drexler,
Michael Kong, Clone House, 1999.

Exquisite precision
CJ Lim

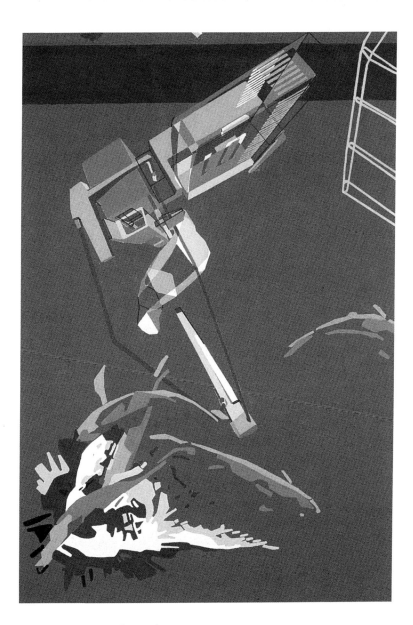

CJ Lim, Ed Lui, Michael Kong,
Paris Searles, Urban Metazoo,
1999.

Notes

1   Peter Cook, 'They
    came to England',
    Artifice, 02, Black
    Dog-Bartlett (London),
    1994.

2   Ibid.

3   Unpublished project
    text supplied by CJ
    Lim, 2000.

4   Ibid.

Of the Metazoo, he writes:

> The sea has borne witness to all the vicissitudes of the coastal city,
> beginning as its lifeblood and finishing as a stagnant dumping ground
> for urban excess. Conceived as a temporary animal sanctuary, the
> Metazoo aims to reclaim the water's edge as a feeding ground for
> migrating geese, simultaneously filtering detritus from the water to
> make it suitable for human activities. The landscape of the shoreline
> reconfigures seasonally, with a series of dockable grids forming a row
> of piers during the winter. During the summer months, the piers
> unfold and float out to trawl the sea and attract hosts, leaving a
> living memory along the coastline.[4]

It doesn't take an architectural genius to observe that Lim's work is immensely
seductive and powerful. This ambitious architect will be on the scene for some
time to come. Architecture needs CJ just like CJ needs architecture.

Technological emancipation

Ron Herron + Simon Herron

I first came across Ron Herron's work in Reyner Banham's book, *Megastructure*.[1] I was just commencing my second year of undergraduate architectural training and *Megastructure* was a revelation: it featured works that were audacious, massively scaled and drawn in ways that challenged the more traditional notations and technologies that I was being taught. This was a cathartic moment for me: I suddenly saw that traditional architectural materials were subject to crippling inertia. The projects of Ron Herron, the other members of Archigram and, of course, Cedric Price, inspired a hope for the future, a future of architectural emancipation brought about by advances in technology. In all these schemes, time was the major component: you don't need things all the time, you change your mind and you respond to fashion, technology and your circumstances. Architecture was a tool you used to facilitate these desires, not an obstacle in their way.

Much of Herron's work has been published, including Walking City (1963) – a project that stalked and free-grazed across continents, perhaps the most famous Archigram image. Here, I feature a project from the latter end of Herron's career, never before published, a design for a ski-jump conceived in conjunction with his son, Simon. Formally, the project is simple and direct. Elements are highly articulated and

Ron Herron and Simon Herron with Ian Liddell, Buro Happold, Arena Bergisel Ski Jump Stadium, Austria, 1990–1. Competition proposal to modify the existing open air stadium to accommodate additional capabilities to extend the life of the arena beyond the short ski-jump season of January. The proposal consists of three principal elements: a convertible roofscape, a facilities wall and new grandstand seating.

Technological emancipation
Ron Herron + Simon Herron

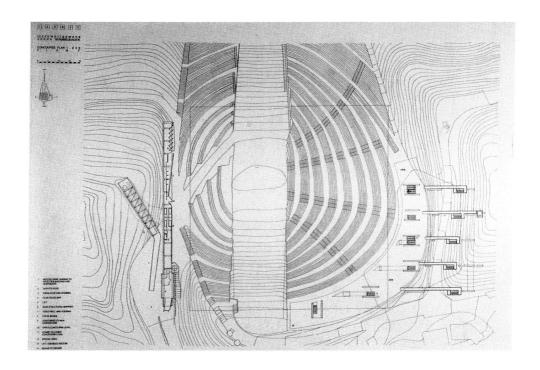

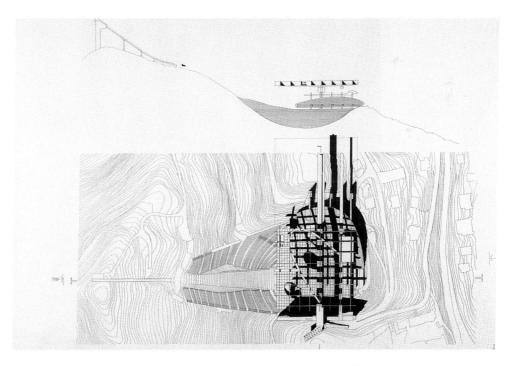

Arena Bergisel Ski Jump Stadium, 1990–1. Top: site plan; bottom: Roof Plan.

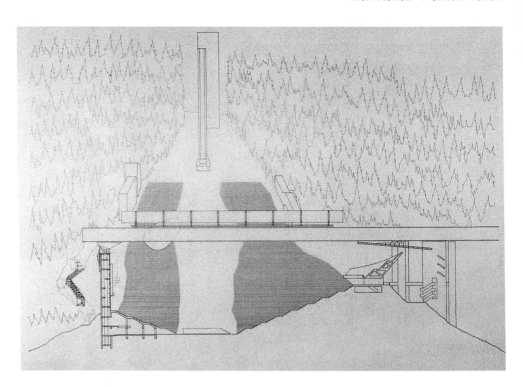

Above and opposite: Ski Jump.

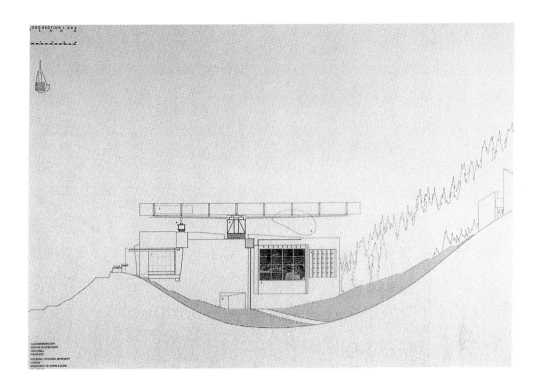

refined; smaller pieces are used to punctuate the larger volumes and their orthogonal structural grid with idiosyncratic marks and geometries. The drawings are characterised by a boldness – the simple declaration of intent that all Herron's work exhibited. He never fiddled with opaque enigma – this was the province of others. These drawings are the work of a master, with a lifetime's experience.

Cedric Price explains better than I do his friend's drawings:

> The drawings of Ron Herron are just such a rarity, and because they are the comprehensive design tool of a uniquely talented person, they become extremely valuable to the beholder. They require no explanation, but demand investigation. They neither swank with visual smartness nor confuse with snobbish obscurantism. They show with minimal effort, unlike their many imitations, the alphabet, rules, manners and potential of the architectural proposals they portray.[2]

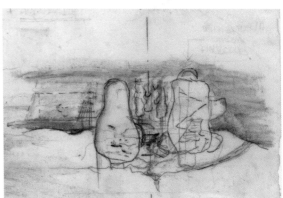

To be born to such a well known father, who, after all was the creator of Oasis (1968), Instant City (1968), Suburban Sets (1974) amongst many other important schemes, and to want to follow him into the architectural profession is a brave thing to do; the mantel is indeed heavy. Simon Herron, however, has kept the Herron name at the forefront of architectural speculation. Like the father, the son is an inspirational teacher. He and his partner Susanna Isa occupy a special piece of architectural terrain: that of small-town but large-landscape America. Not for them the glitz of cosmopolitan USA; they prefer cowboy boots and bomb test grounds. Their interest lies where the desert meets nuclear silos, where B52 graveyards meet alcohol-fuelled rednecks and where sequinned Elvises meet black-gold southwestern America.

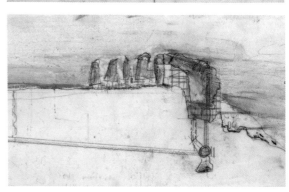

The younger Herron's AA thesis project was the Weather Station (1990). It shows the same assured drafting style, the same interest in emancipating inflatables, in taut-skin technology and armaturing steel structure of his father's work. These preoccupations have since been augmented by

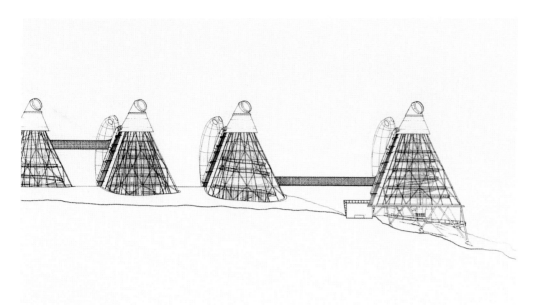

Above and opposite:
Simon Herron, Weather
Station, Oslo, Norway, 1988.
Located on the outskirts of
Oslo the project presents five
figures; towards the city
iridescent pneumatic skins
mimic sky colour, in the
extremes of winter protective
overcoats are worn, backs
turned against the Northern
winds.

Herron/Isa's other notions about impermanent poetics, the play of the pheno-menology of landscape, the differing timescale of natural architectonic pieces like trees and plants, and their love of the surreal commercial aberrations like 10-storey high cowboys or other crass simulacra. The Weather Station shows little of these, though they were already gestating: ideas of shimmer, of diurnal juxtaposi-tions and just plain fun. Fun is a crucial component to the Herron/Isa practice, Velvetair, fun and optimism. We should end with another quote from Cedric Price, written about Ron Herron but equally true of his son.

This brings one to the major strength of Herron's work – namely optimism and delight related to the future, the possible, the desirable, and yes, the better. There is an unashamed delight in fiddling with what is and producing something new. It is never a question of merely improving the present and indeed no real architecture is. We are neither dentists nor beauticians. Herron's strength is that his architecture is refined and defined within his drawings but leaves open the possibility of further improvement by those who observe. Transposing 'user' for 'observer' in the case of the built – that is exactly what architecture should do.[3]

Notes

1   Reyner Banham, *Megastructure*, Thames & Hudson (London), 1976.

2   Cedric Price, *Introduction to Ron Herron: 20 Years of Drawing*, AA Publications (London), 1980.

3   Ibid.

Lyrical mechanism

Christine Hawley

Christine Hawley's work is always fastidious. Yet behind an extraordinary consistency of product, it has never been exempt from the *Zeitgeist*; often it has been influential in forming that *Zeitgeist*. Peter Cook, Hawley's long-time collaborator, fleshes out some historical detail:

> One of the most talented offspring of our own corner – a territory that
> I have frequently referred to as 'lyrical mechanism' – was
> characteristically English in her combination of inner toughness and
> outer reticence. But it is hard for me to describe Christine Hawley
> simply, not least because her character has emerged in a series of
> imperceptible shifts over the twenty years that I have known her.
> For Christine came to architecture after having nearly become a

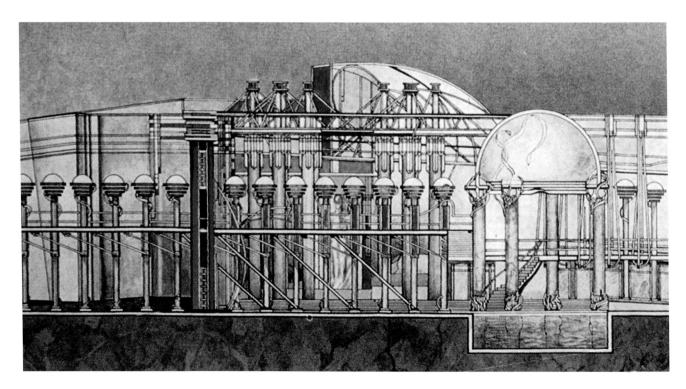

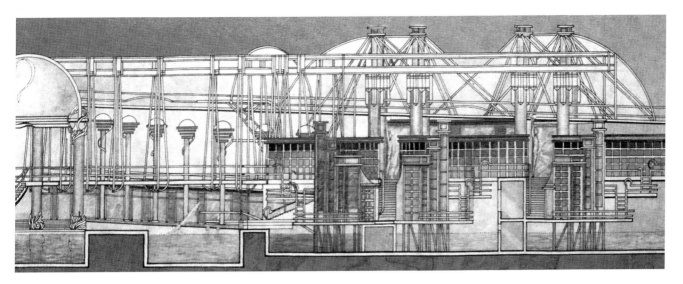

painter – something not uncommon in England. Training at one of
London's most academic girls' schools had not prepared her for the
free-fall atmosphere of the AA in the 1970s, but it did enable the
painter to emerge through a wayward mechanism encouraged by her
teacher of four years, Ron Herron. As she has developed as a teacher
herself, this mixture of the disciplined mind and the billowing line
came forth as a basis for her aesthetic.[1]

Hawley's time as a student at the AA culminated in the project for the Porchester
Baths in London (1978). It foresaw the High-tech fetishisation of the tension cable
yet understood that the historicist continuity of architecture was something that
could still be grist to the creative mill. Hawley posited an architecture that flirted
with the mechanised detail but swathed it in commodious, sumptuous decadence.
The project was beautifully drawn and became one of the defining moments of
the post-Archigram AA. The drawings reek of an experiential architecture, an architecture of explicit choreographed incidence, elegant formal games and kinky
detailing. The scheme is almost Victorian, and reminds one of the University
Museum, Oxford (Thomas Deane and Benjamin Woodward, 1855–60), not because
of its vitalistic detailing or its Ruskinian honouring of craftsmanship but for its
stringent ordering of structure. A near contemporary project was Alsop and Lyall's
Riverside Studios (London, 1982), which shared the wayward tendril, and the
strangely postmodern references but lacked the sheer delicacy that Hawley brought
to her scheme.

Another project that illustrates a shift in Hawley's formal preferences is the Stained
Glass Museum, Frankfurt 1986 (in collaboration with Peter Cook). The museum
is basically a symmetrical plan, which allows its central staircase and circulation
space to skew. Ancillary accommodation is a cacophony of unruly plan forms that
jostle for position to one side of the otherwise mute box of the museum. This
suggested muteness is in stark contrast to Porchester Baths, which, with its baro-
quely engineered complexity, is a little raver. The Stained Glass Museum is a simple
building designed in a complex way. Small pieces become important, whether it

is the signifying armatures of the entrance or the cabal of spaces clustered under its neat apron. It is a project that is naughtily contrived and contrary, masked in the sensible.

Another actually built contemporary piece from the Cook and Hawley stable was the Berlin Housing block (1985). Again, it utilised the tactic of the sticky-out bit and the finely chiselled modernist volume in artful contrast to one another.

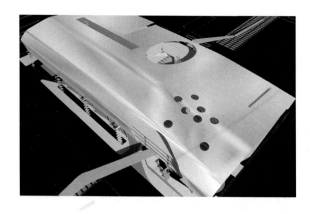

In the 1990s, Hawley's work veered from the almost Corbusian aesthetic of the original sections of the Gifu Housing in Japan – a project that was built in 1994 and continues – to an interest in the sleek, seamless skin of, for example, the Congress Centre EUR in Rome of 1998. Here, we can quote from Hawley's design report for the project:

> The scale of the building makes it important to establish its identity externally, the skin is deliberately simple and the surface is only broken by significant points of public entry and to indicate the presence of more significant events within the building.

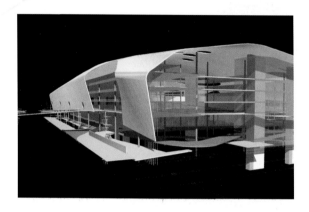

Above and below: Congress Centre EUR, Rome, 1998.

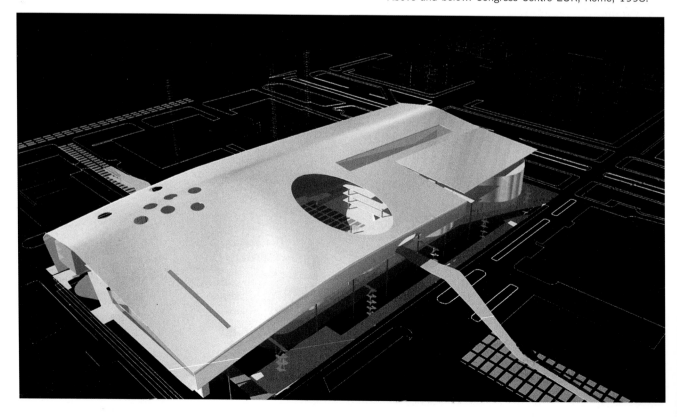

Lyrical mechanism
Chrstine Hawley

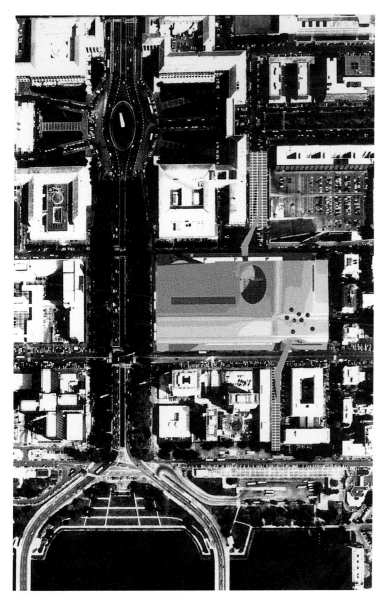

Congress Centre, EUR, Rome, 1998.

The major spaces within the congress centre are both distinctive formally and in size and the building is a seamless skin, it is clear at the lower levels through which the sculptural forms and volumes of the main spaces are recognised.

The building is seen as part of an urban continuum that both connects and unites the EUR district. It was important that the hall was conspicuously integrated into the working infrastructure of the area. To this end, the internal organisation of the piazza areas echoes both the orthogonal geometry of the city and the principle that the building should continue a sequence of urban spaces. The public piazzas within the building are essentially of the twenty-first century, but both adhere to and reinterpret the historic model.[2]

With Hawley, what on the surface seem cool, rationally argued schemes, conceal extreme formal and spatial audacities, but always embedded in historical precedent and the detail of the immediate *genius loci*. This is her strength; her avant-gardism is cloaked in a carefully formulated logic, always ready to explain and convince without pressure or ego.

Notes

1   Peter Cook, 'They Came to England', *Artifice*, 02, Black Dog-Bartlett (London), 1994.

2   Christine Hawley, Architects' Competition documentation, 1998.

Things worth seeing

William Firebrace

William Firebrace's work has an enigmatic beauty that ranges from the considerably abstract to wonderfully drawn and rendered perspectives, axonometrics and cartoons. I use the word 'cartoons' not in a pejorative way but in the sense of work that is the declaration of architectural intent and a trial of compositional placement.

I first became aware of Firebrace's work in 1983 through his competition entry for Opera de la Bastille, Paris. This project had stunning audacity, was brimming with theatrical ideas and ambience and was just plain weird. The drawings have a virtuoso feeling; they mostly eschew traditional architectural representational projections, pulling one into a cacophony of rampant objects, some small, some auditorium sized. The scheme was an attempt to blow away the mystique of the Opera, to democratise it, yet to imbue it with even more of the business of show. This was achieved by making visible what goes on in opera houses. So much of opera's theatre is hidden from the boxed-up viewer's eyes. In the context of this project, ignorance is far from bliss.

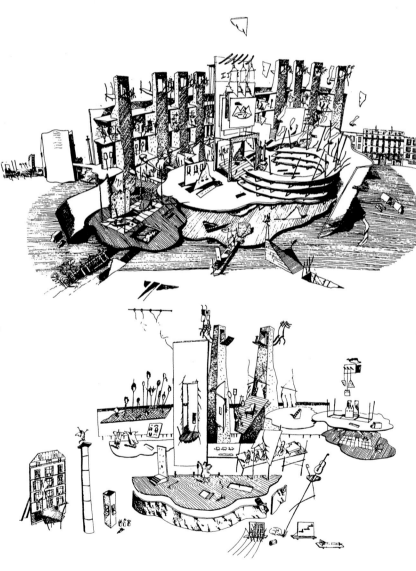

Opera de la Bastille, 1983.

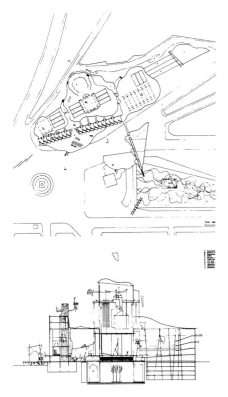

Opera de la Bastille, 1983.
Above: plan and section;
right: urban massing.

In Firebrace's own words:

the design of the Opera House and its relationship with the surrounding city is based on three premises. First, the Opera is to be a series of stages, so that all those entering it will be to some extent both spectator and performer. The smallest stage is that of the make-up table, at which the singers observe themselves and their transformation into the role they are about to play; the largest stage is that of the Place de la Bastille itself, on which singers can watch, from balconies in the facades, the citizens of Paris and their vehicles endlessly circulating. In between are foyer areas, on which the opera spectators observe one another, and the actual theatrical stages, where the audience finally encounters the singers. Second, the Opera House should be capable of mounting external performances, transforming the Place de la Bastille into an enormous set, in particular during the proposed celebration of 1989. Finally, the most exciting part of the theatre is always the backstage area – sets, ropes, backcloths and stage machinery. This proposal exposes this

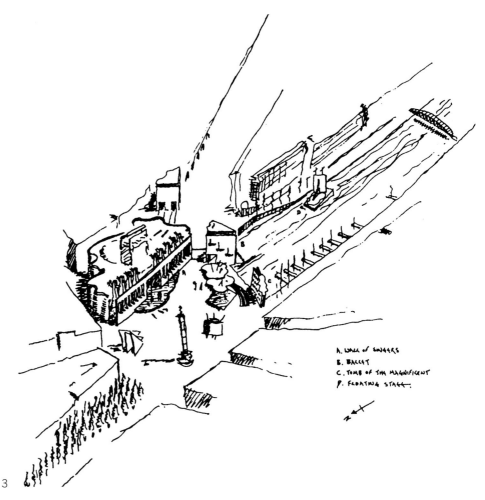

3

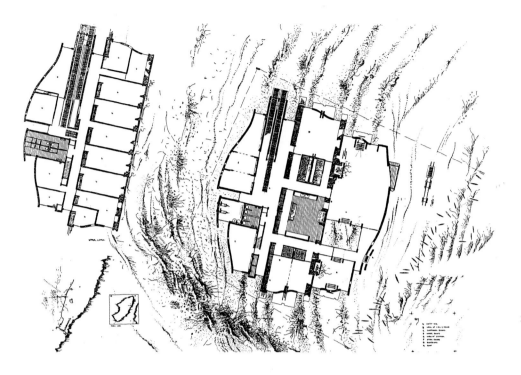

Pilgrim shelter, Isola Iona,
Scotland, 1987. Left: plan;
below: built up vertical
building strata.

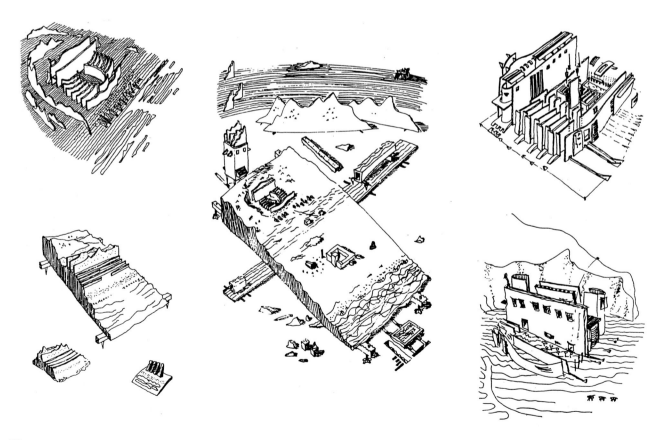

area to public view, so that the public areas are penetrated by the ascending and descending stage sets, the theatrical stages being reduced to spaces where the sets come to rest, a temporary meeting place for audience, singers and musicians.[1]

Firebrace's architectural lexicon is composed of the considered placement of pieces, which are often surreal, allegorical and figurative, in relation to a figured, cut and slotted, elevated and paletted ground plane. His symbolic language is borne out of each project anew. Always highly advanced, esoteric and spectacular, it is composed of both rationalist and expressionistic architectural motifs. His work does not dwell in technological arenas, and it is surprising to find that he once worked in Richard Rogers' office. To him, technology is simply a means to an end.

Firebrace's competition entry for Isola Iona, Scotland (1987), which proposed a shelter for pilgrims staying on the island, is introduced by frenzied and expressive drawings hinting at the site's individuality, its pre-Cambrian rocks, its geological faults, extreme weather, earthworks and wild untamable beauty. His initial gambit was to lay a series of conceptual lines upon the earth to create a complex of linear enclosures. These striations of space mimic the layered geometry of the ground. Indeed, Firebrace further explores the project by creating a suite of drawings that take some of their tactics from the notations of geomorphologists and physical geographers. Having established these tactics, he then erodes the clean architectural strata and breaks one into another, allowing space to flow more freely yet in a highly choreographed way. The result is a stunning progression of spaces, which are fully articulated and integrated with their landscape.

Chepstow Castle, Wales.

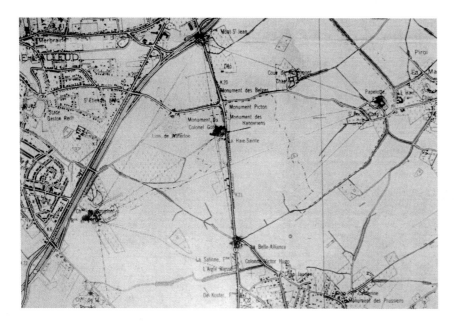

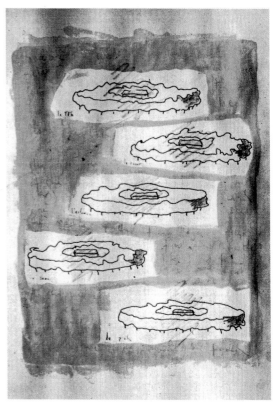

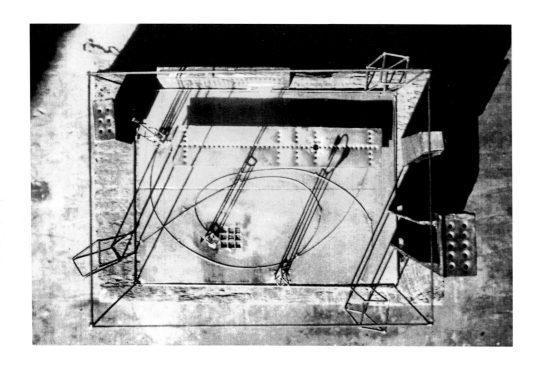

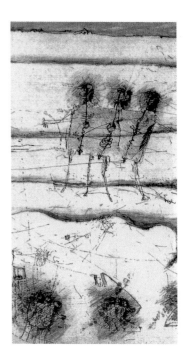

Another fine project, 'Five Anatomical Rooms' of 1989, oscillates around five farms on the site of the Battle of Waterloo. Specifically, these sites are Goumant, La Haie-Saint, Mont St Jean, La Belle Alliance and Papelotte. Firebrace describes the project:

> A landscape in Belgium, a former battle ground. Napoleon, Wellington, Blucher. Triple armies have roamed across the farmland, their soldiers killed in canon fire and cavalry charge. Now no trace of their passage is visible. The land is occupied by farm machines and cattle. Beside each farm is a planted wood. Each wood is of a different tree: oak, chestnut, beech, ash, maple. Within each wood is a constructed room, raised slightly from the ground on metal bearers. The walls of the rooms are formed of metal panels, shone brightly on the outside and lined with red-painted timber on the inside. The floor is of polished wood. Each room contains three oversize metal chairs, mounted on tracks. They move from locations within the walls to three positions: the pit, the table and the window. A point of entry is provided, with two small doors on the outside and two large doors on the inside: also a wine rack and a wc. The room is lit from three light slots in the ceiling; the slots mirror the tracks of the chairs. Each of the woods grow at a different rate. When a wood is fully grown, the room is removed. Within the woods there remains only the space the rooms have occupied.[2]

Firebrace is also an architectural teacher and sets an example of what any right-minded teacher wants for their students. That is, to become sensitive to site and the evolving language of architecture, and to create work that is idiosyncratically personal and courageous. He has ploughed a highly original field in architectural discourse and one can only hope that his experimentation and expeditions continue to gain momentum. Architects like Firebrace are crucial to architecture's continued health and vitality.

Opposite: Five Anatomical Rooms, Waterloo, Belgium, 1989. Clockwise from top left: site plane; concept drawing; detail of room; detail of a field.

Notes

1   William Firebrace, unpublished information made available to the author, 2000.

2   Ibid.

New mythologies for urban mechanisms

Neil Denari

Every time I sit on a plane and look out over the wing on to the tarmac of the runway I think of Neil Denari. It's not the wing I'm examining but the markings on the ground: lines, chevrons, diagonal hatchings and large sweeping painted arcs – techno-hieroglyphics. In 1987, Princeton Architectural Press published a seminal little book in the 'Pamphlet Architecture' series called *Building Machines*. The most audacious and inspiring work within this book was by Neil Denari. Three of his projects were featured: Monastery, New York City No 8305 (1983); Solar Clock, London, No 8602 (1986) and Adams House (in Paradise), New York City, No 8407 (1984). Some of the other works featured in the book had an even more explicitly mechanistic aesthetic than Denari's, but his work also explored another space, it had more than one string to its bow, it set itself more difficult tasks with more lyrical briefs. With Denari, the machinic does not sacrifice all its sights on the altar of empiricism.

Below and opposite: Monastery, New York City, No 8305, 1983.

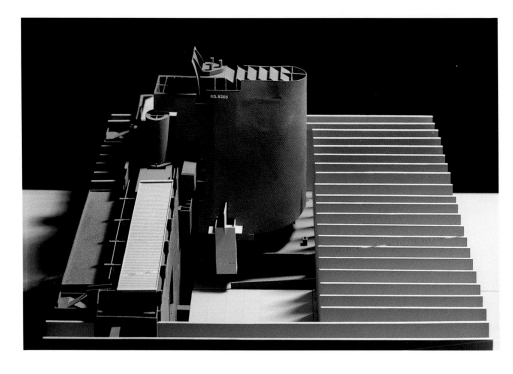

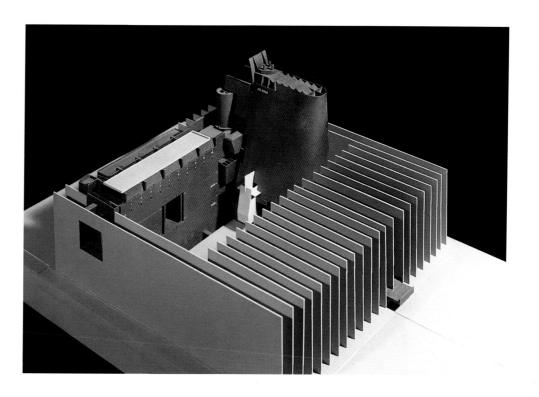

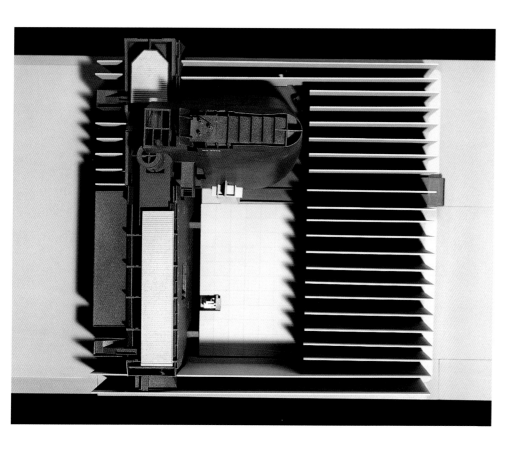

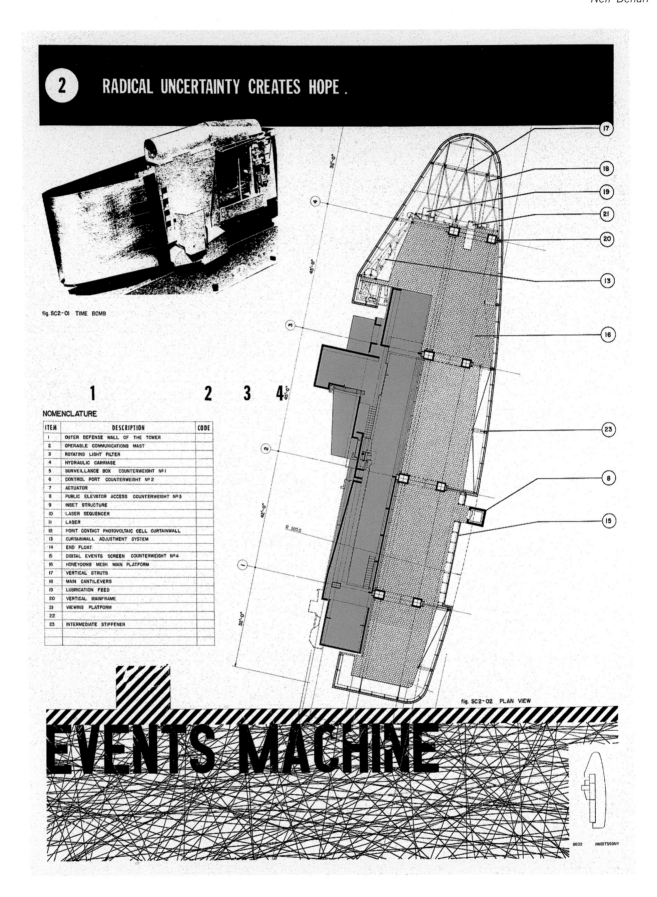

2 RADICAL UNCERTAINTY CREATES HOPE.

fig. SC2-01 TIME BOMB

NOMENCLATURE

ITEM	DESCRIPTION	CODE
1	OUTER DEFENSE WALL OF THE TOWER	
2	OPERABLE COMMUNICATIONS MAST	
3	ROTATING LIGHT FILTER	
4	HYDRAULIC CARRIAGE	
5	SURVEILLANCE BOX COUNTERWEIGHT Nº1	
6	CONTROL PORT COUNTERWEIGHT Nº2	
7	ACTUATOR	
8	PUBLIC ELEVATOR ACCESS COUNTERWEIGHT Nº3	
9	INSET STRUCTURE	
10	LASER SEQUENCER	
11	LASER	
12	POINT CONTACT PHOTOVOLTAIC CELL CURTAINWALL	
13	CURTAINWALL ADJUSTMENT SYSTEM	
14	END FLOAT	
15	DIGITAL EVENTS SCREEN COUNTERWEIGHT Nº4	
16	HONEYCOMB MESH MAIN PLATFORM	
17	VERTICAL STRUTS	
18	MAIN CANTILEVERS	
19	LUBRICATION FEED	
20	VERTICAL MAINFRAME	
21	VIEWING PLATFORM	
22		
23	INTERMEDIATE STIFFENER	

fig. SC2-02 PLAN VIEW

EVENTS MACHINE

He describes the monastery project in these terms:

> The monastery, as a valuable contemporary programme, is a refuge
> from the progressive exhaustion of the metropolis, a place where
> spirit and thinking are separated from but are reflective of the city
> itself. As a collapsible set of realities, described in a process of scalar
> reductionism – from the infinite, Cartesian world of the city to the
> smallest cell – the intention is to relinquish our usual mental habitat,
> to suspend for any length of time the normal processes in favour of a
> more contemplative one. The monastery is machine as it mediates
> the energy between man and Deity, thus claiming the mechanistic
> quality by converting energy not into work but into Being.[1]

Denari's chosen tactic of representation for this set of projects is powerful and
artfully composed, with plan, section, elevation and perspective juxtaposed, yet
only just – no chaotic sublimity for him. Denari's sublime is premeditated and
specific. The monastery does not fall into the trap of mechanistic determinism and
coerces the reader into imagining strange mechanised ritual within its vessel-like
spaces. Conversely, it stretches our understanding of liturgy as we attempt to reconcile it with the shadowy muscularity of the monastery's constitution.

The Solar Clock project was conceived to skirt around the battlements of the
medieval fortress, the Tower of London. Its skin included a solar curtain that could
utilise 30 percent of the sun's available energy. Again, the project's aspirations
range further afield than just the mechanistic:

Solar Clock, No 8602,
London, 1986.

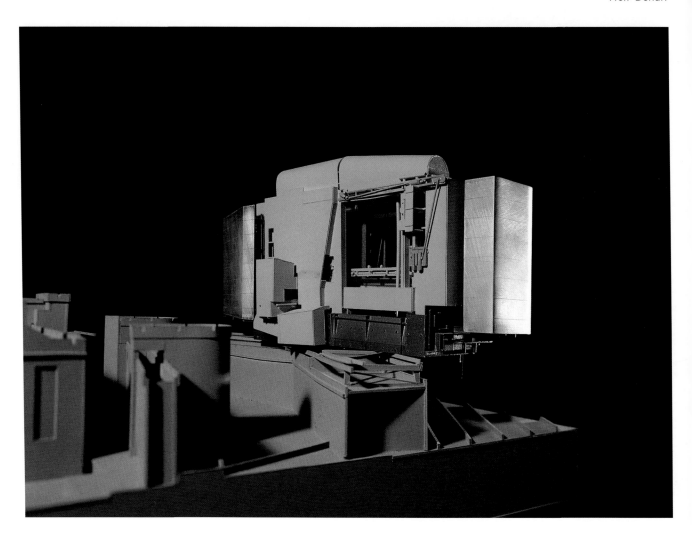

To make a Husserlian description of collaboration between TIME and the MACHINE is obvious. The machine may be considered as *in* the world yet displaced in turn by its almost daily modification. This continuous, almost self-perpetuating regeneration speaks of the *now* of the machine, describing technology's development as inevitable as time itself. However, the *intentionality* of the machine, as an *a priori* programme, is often misdirected by two major forces, (1) a subversion through proliferation, and (2) invalid intentions.

Solar Clock, London, No 8602, 1986.

The machinic world of Neil Denari is much more readable in his early work. In recent years, his practice has been more concerned with the shifting topology of technologised space, the folding of 'world surfaces', the codification of space and the blurring of the wall/floor divide. His extremely robust and elegant works have adopted the hyperreal exactitude of the computer, with less space for enigma. The computer is the ultimate machine; a machine made to mimic other machines and to take over their identity. The computer relies on the virtual machine within; it can become CD-ROM player, video screen, typewriter and calculator with the click of a mouse. As the machine almost disappears, its imperative being towards soft-ness and invisibility, Denari's work has in turn become less overtly mechanistic.

Back to 1987. Denari's Solar Clock resonates with older, more arcane notions, practices and mythologies:

> The solar day, whose measure of time is based on a single rotation of
> the earth, is described in a new way via the circumnavigation by this
> clock machine of the Tower of London. Set upon the outer defence
> wall of the Tower, riding on a rail-set inserted into the existing
> structure, the object completes one loop around the site in 24 hours.
> It is a machine of approximation, a grounding of the SUN in the city
> of London.

Here we see an urge to develop and re-express the city's relationship to nature's mystic rhythms. Denari has posited a contemporary Stonehenge in the image of the machine with the spatial and invasive tactics of a Trojan Horse. 'Is scientific inference the (only) basis for generating information? Do buildings then amount to huge pieces of scientific apparatus?' he asks. In these early projects, with their chambers of contemplation, sacred vessels and cyclic reconciliation, the ghost within the machine is that of alchemy. It is at this point in Denari's career that myth meets machine, ritual meets rationalism and Futurism meets symbol; these intersections give a vitality to the work that is infectious.

It is interesting that these studies were conducted on the eve of the computer's rise to ubiquity. They provide a snap-shot of the last fling of the heroic mecha-nism in the halcyon period before reality was snatched away bit by bit and architecture was forced to consider the virtual. A collector's item to be sure.

Notes

1   Neil Denari quoted in Robert McCarter (ed), *Building Machines*, Princeton
     Architectural Press (New York), 1987. All subsequent quotations are from this source.

Dynamic heterogeneity

Decq and Cornette

I always think of Odile Decq and Benoît Cornette as belonging to a small constituency that can be referred to as 'humane high-tech'. The work of this French practice does not display the bloody-minded obsession and 'sodyouesque' quality of some of the more visible, English, high-tech posturing. It is pluralist, not dogmatic. There are no cosmetics, no unnecessary Baroque details. The philosophy of Decq and Cornette is part and parcel of its aesthetic; some might define it as 'appropriatism'. Another architect with the same sense of appropriateness is Ian Ritchie. His work on the house at Eagle Rock (1985) attained a desirable synthesis of dogma, symbol and identity of place.

The French practice has made successful urban housing that bases its success on the dissolution of the High-tech palette. Domesticity requires many unique considerations, which include smallness of scale, identity of place, and privacy. This is one area in which the finely tuned world of High-tech is sadly lacking. Decq and Cornette, however, understands what Peter Cook has pointed out: 'architecture of the future has to come to grips with theatre, atmosphere, seductiveness, tactility . . . we just can't sit back on cerebral diagrams, however clever, we can't just sit back on mathematics'.[1]

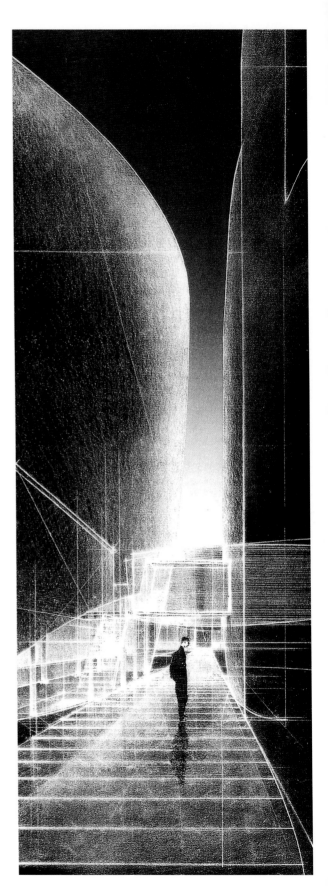

Right and opposite:
Amenagement du site Francis Poulenc, Tours.

Decq and Cornette is well aware of the technological imperative and the need for its continuous exploitation to find new ways to create architecture:

> Today's society is caught in a moment of complexity
> and acceleration. Speed, movement and displacement
> have changed our vision of space, cities and landscape.
> The rapid development of communication networks
> compresses time to such an extent that we can no
> longer build up a clear image of the city or of the living
> space. We are all nomads, travelling between reality and
> unreality. Moving from city to city, sending faxes,
> channel surfing, tele-conferencing are all means by
> which we navigate space and meaning. This
> globalisation of our society, through the mechanisms of
> information exchange and travel exchange, reconfigures
> our comprehension of space in motion. The architecture
> of these new territories could therefore be perceived as
> imperfect, unlimited and evolving. Cities and territories
> are becoming redefined as a network in continuous
> flux.[2]

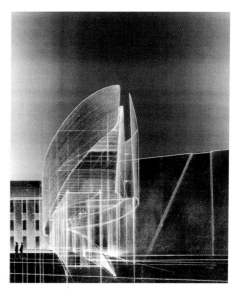

The growth of a mechanistic urban syntax has attracted scant attention. In 1984, Ron Herron and Jan Kaplicky introduced their unit at the AA in urban terms:

> The current debate on urbanism lists, amongst others,
> the street, public square, perimeter block, the idea of
> the city as extended rooms and a regard for historical
> and spatial continuity . . . These are elements that can
> be reinterpreted through wit and invention rather than
> being merely a regurgitation of the Classical or
> Modernist models.[3]

Decq and Cornette is developing such urban models. The practice is not only experienced in the traditional set-piece urban architecture, but is also able to create urban flow, urban mix and spatial sequence. Decq and Cornette has described its creative thought patterns as follows:

> The necessity of displacement and the movement of the
> body inside space must be integrated. A succession of
> points of view generates a dynamic vision of space. The

Below and opposite: Triangle de la Folie, La Defense, Paris.

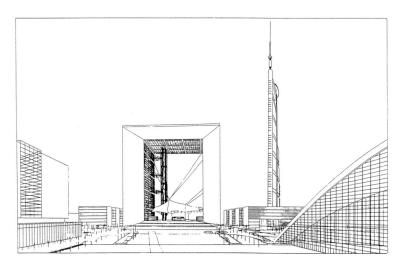

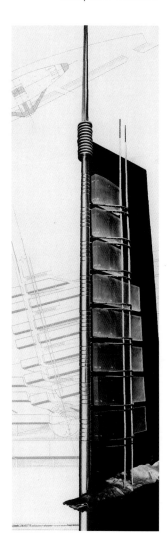

variation of perspectives creates a permanent tension and a sensual, complex ambiguity in the perception of space. The sequential circulation of images such as linear distortion constantly displaces and disturbs one point of view. We never think in terms of centred space and axes, but in terms of sliding and tangential spaces, of chains of images, to create escaping lines, moving perspectives, sequential images where tension is introduced in the assemblage of fading forms. Architecture and space are a matter of constant discovery and nothing is ever out of bounds.[4]

In an image-addicted world, Decq and Cornette's attempt to create these 'chains of images' to define, contain and give coherency, should be applauded. So often, architects forget that our art is one of spatial manipulation, and as a result become caught in the images of their work and consequently the image of themselves.

90

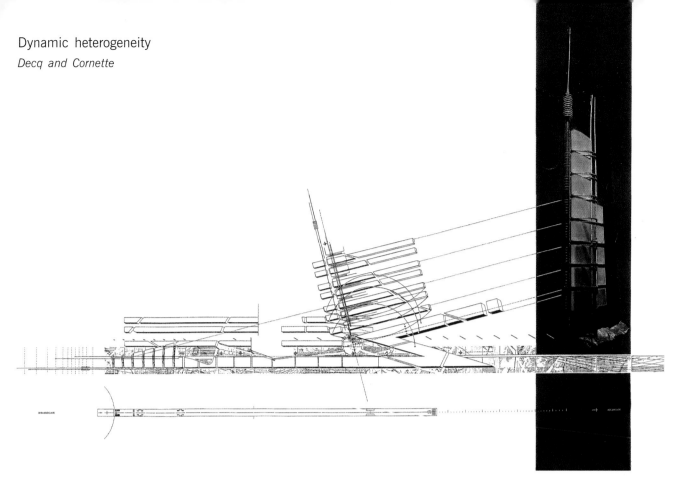

This tendency is the beginning of the end and should be fought tooth and claw. Decq and Cornette's architecture does not trade off tired and defunct formulae of aesthetics or form but seeks an original solution to the particular urban problem on the board at the time. Every project is different; every project is experimental: no ubiquitous sheds for this practice.

Decq and Cornette's work is at once expressive and urbane. It is a beacon in the normally conservative French architectural scene. Sometimes, the practice suffers because of what the French see as an extreme stance. To English eyes, its work is sensitive, well considered and inclusive. The practice is at a transition point and I for one wish it and its Gothic frontwoman Odile Decq well. Difference is the lifeblood of the architectural profession. To attempt to quash it is a crime against humanity, society and culture. Decq and Cornette is a necessary irritant in its homeland, which I hope will learn to honour its assets better.

Notes

1   Peter Cook, 'The Architecture of Optimism', lecture at the RIBA, 4 December 1979.

2   Decq and Cornette in Neil Spiller and Peter Cook (eds), *Power of Contemporary Architecture*, Wiley-Academy (London), 1999.

3   Jan Kaplicky and Ron Herron, Diploma Unit 8, AA Prospectus, 1984.

4   *Power of Contemporary Architecture*, op cit.

Thoughts at the datum of understanding

Jean Michel Crettaz

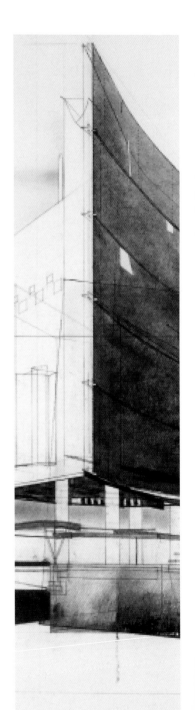

Peter Wilson's teaching and work have had a huge impact on the 1980s and the projects in this book. One of the ways Jean Michel Crettaz's projects are interesting is that they illustrate Peter Wilson's AA unit at the close of the 1980s.

In a conversation with Crettaz, he described his drawings as 'datums of understanding' or as 'horizons of thoughts'. At the time I didn't know what he meant. He lent me probably 200 or more drawings, competition entries, work from Cooper Union, or the Architectural Association. He is an enigmatic character and the drawings are equally mysterious though highly specific. They are almost Hejdukian but not; almost Wilsonian but not. Much is made of the perched armature and the clustered multiple object. Much is also made of the horizon; its truncated datum is everywhere and it is not always horizontal. Perspectives are low-slung, with the distortion dial on max. Viewpoints are vastly important and ever changing. The architectonic interventions and their rotations sometimes float in a sea of colour – often a peaty brown. This tactic defines numerous spatial fields on to the two-dimensional plane of the drawing. Crettaz's objects always negotiate the terrain through and within these fields.

These objects are often conic or have inclined surface envelopes. They are auditorium shaped with various levels of angularity. Other objects are extruded towards the horizon and are accompanied by splintered fragments. The objects seem to have a special gravity that contorts the picture plane. Armatures are more often or not intricate and delicate and sometimes lash out, tracing an arc of influence. Enclosures frequently receive images from projectors both within and without. Objects tend to dig deep into the ground plane; supporting rails or beams – opportunities for more perching of idiosyncratic architectural owls – are embedded deep into the land. Crettaz's mechanisms and mannerisms are not late-twentieth century archetypes; they are not engineered with *fin de siècle* exactitude. Leonardo would feel at home with their Artesian screws, cams and wooden-cogged gearage.

Thoughts at the datum of understanding

Jean Michel Crettaz

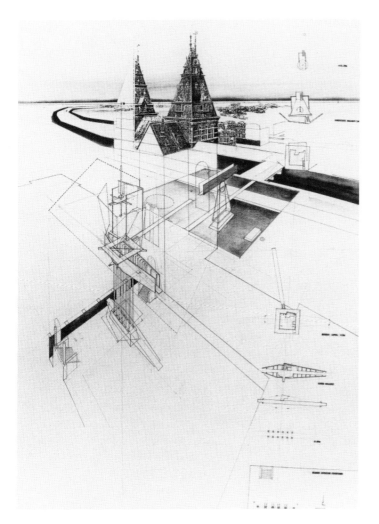

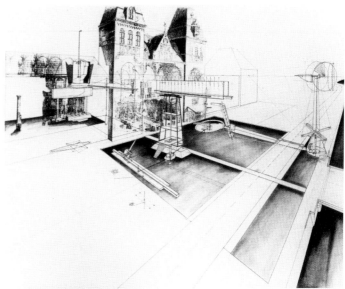

'Jean Michel's Crettaz's work
is highly enigmatic; captions
attempt to condense meaning.'

This is how Crettaz himself describes his London-Tokyo scheme (1990), which attempted to synthesise in to London the urban conditions of Tokyo, including fast construction techniques and issues of scale:

> The architectural project is specific, dealing with the physical and psychological limitation and expansion of space. It is set in the Hayward Gallery [London]. An attachment similar to that previously on the body [an infinite conic prosthetic] was added to the building. This was how it was perceived: I ascended the stairs, I could feel the stairs entering my body by sections into the building. Inside it was dark, the walls tapered inwards and I could not move forward, I turned. The cones of light from the facing wall pulled me forward. I peered through the holes from which they came and saw three objects in the great white space. People spiralled around the objects at various speeds and varying distances. Compared to the objects, the people moved distractedly. A few metres beyond the outer wall of the gallery a rotating mirror was capturing views. I saw myself and

Above and opposite:
London – Tokyo, 1990;
composite drawing.

Thoughts at the datum of understanding
Jean Michel Crettaz

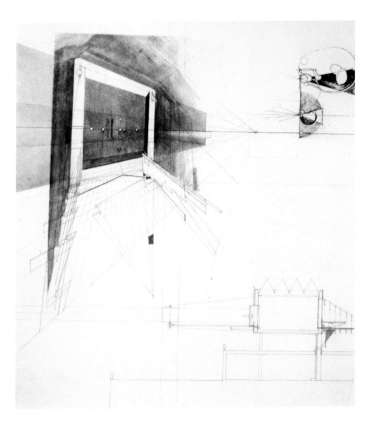

the gallery behind me in one of the fractions that made up the panorama.[1]

So it seems that Crettaz's world is one of orbits and incidents connected to the relative position of the viewer. One feels that he still sees all this work as mobile or creatively fluid. Like his projects, he is forever on the move, adjusting to new positions. He seems to enjoy the radial, shifting placement and juxtaposition of pieces, creating dances of effortless parallax for his amusement. He draws in a way that can dazzle the eye and the mind.

I have refrained from discussing Crettaz's work in programmatic or functional terms, not because it is limited in this respect but because of its latent poetry and spirit. One does not need to explain; one has to examine the photographic evidence. In an essay of November 1990, Crettaz wrote:

Liz Diller gave us a programme. Included as illustrations were Leonardo Da Vinci's and Oscar Schlemmer's depictions of the human body. Amongst Diller's words was the statement 'As we cannot escape the presence of the human body, it is being submitted to you as photographic evidence'.

I faced my life-sized 'photographic evidence'; words from Virgil's *Aeneid* came to mind: 'The spirit supports from within: infused through its every member, mind sets the mass in motion and mingles itself with the mighty body.' I painted over my 'evidence' and to the body I added an attachment for infinite conic perception.[2]

Notes

1   Jean Michel Crettaz, unpublished portfolio notes.

2   Ibid.

Arcadian architecture

Peter Cook

Peter Cook has more 'lost' projects than most. However, while they are 'lost' in the sense that they are often unbuilt, they have frequently been published. Cook has been at the vanguard against architectural stasis, a mentor to many and the encourager of a selection of the weirdest architects on the planet.

Cook often describes his love\hate relationship with countryside. He was not born in a large city but I have never heard him express the wish to get away from it all for a weekend in the country. Cities are his natural habitat; he keeps the cognitive maps of many of the world's cities in his head, remembering them by the position of their restaurants and notable architecture. However, he often shows

Layer City, 1984.

Arcadian architecture
Peter Cook

Layer City, 1984.

slides of vegetation growing over things, giving them another mask or organic skin. He calls these 'veg' or 'growies'. I once heard him use these expressions in front of a very self-important landscape architect who could not restrain a snort of disgust.

If you asked him, I suspect he would say he believed in modern architecture and in the technological modernist project. He admires the Smithsons, for example, but also has a passing acquaintance with the technology of the Jetsons. I believe Cook to be a different type of modern architect. He is an architect with a propensity for flamboyant catholic taste. His preoccupations far exceed the guilty crap of the modernists.

As is well known, his work of the 1960s was more up and down, more plug in, drop out, more do anything, anywhere, anytime – visionary, critically acclaimed, hijacked by the High-tech knights and made corporately acceptable. But Cook moved on to another more formal romanticism. It is this work of the 1980s and early 1990s that I wish to illustrate here.

Cook's big ideas, which he always numbers, have now reached the mid-forties and can be organised chronologically. In 1985, the Architectural Association in London held a retrospective exhibition of his work entitled '21 Years – 21 Ideas'. The show was flamboyantly colourful in contrast to the usual timid exhibits of most architects. Its inventiveness was breathtaking, especially to a student like me from a provincial polytechnic. The work imbued the viewer with a sense of 'anything

Left: Skyglade Westhafen, 1986;
below: Skywaft City, 1985;
bottom: Way Out West, 1988.

is possible' and suggested an affirmative answer to a question that over the years has become more urgent: is it possible to create environments that are more integrated hybrids of the rural and the urban?

Patrick Reyntiens – interestingly, the author of the definitive stained-glass book – reviewed the exhibition in the *AA Files* journal in Autumn 1985:

> This is a Rabelaisian show; the idiom of the day and the assumed ideas behind it are taken up, dissected, turned about, explored, exposed and represented as a phantasmagoric nightmare of transposed ideas. The British, for all their humour, don't like being set up. Twenty years ago it was the irreverence of Archigram which alienated the pundits of Queen Anne's Gate. Such licentious irresponsibility and exuberance were not of the order of the Modern Movement. That was a serious, functional, staid, and essentially puritanical dominance over the British, making fun with an elephantine footsy on the South Bank and flattening the public's instinct for enjoyment.[1]

The projects of the 1980s include Layer City, Studio Tower for Frankfurt, and Skywaft City. Cook's work around this time was concerning itself with the urban scale and the master planning of cities. Specifically, it was a series of drawn essays about the nature of the city and its extraordinary capacity for metamorphosis and self reinvention. Cook was also trying to develop scenarios and metamorphic districts that would do nothing to inhibit the eclectic taste of the urban dweller of the future. His cities were Arcadian, encouraging a healthy interest in the conservatory, the roof garden and the window box. But in Cook's world, these usually small concessions to the natural quickly go out of control and start to infiltrate the harder parts of the architecture. These works always situate themselves on the thin line between fantasy, straight urban planning, Baroque extravagance and fun.

Cook is an obsessive; he lives, breathes and eats architecture. But his obsession is not to do with getting one idea right, as with many of his peers; it is about the continual search for new ideas – ideas that push the envelope of what architecture might be able to do for us.

Another concern that seems to permeate his work is the choreography of translucence: many of the projects have envelopes or skins that play with opacity, whether in the use of meshes, vegetation or even clouds. A 1981 drawing entitled 'The Outriders of Layer City – drawn in Oslo and inspired by North Sea Cities and Christine Hawley's Porchester Baths' is captioned in the *AA Files* review of '21 Years – 21 Ideas': 'Like the Eddystone Lighthouse – Winstanley's version – the topless cloud – capped towers rise in an atmosphere of serenity and self-consciousness'. Returning to the text itself:

> There is one other attribute which allows the drawings to escape
> from the present utilitarian impasse: the atmosphere of leisure that
> pervades the majority of the buildings depicted in the drawings . . .
> The art of leisure was well understood until the advent of the steam
> engine. From that time, it became not the norm of a healthy society,
> which it should be, but a thrust – a side indulgence, sop to a hard-
> working population. A leisured society was always a cultured society,
> and those decadent French abbes and obscenely rich Austrian
> archbishops, who knew how to while away their leisure hours
> profitably, inevitably commissioned the right architects to give
> expression to their day-dreams.

With Cook, work seems to replace leisure. But to him, work does not hold that Victorian implication of defeat, but a sense of fun, exploration, messy play and, in amongst all of this, craftsmanship. For Cook is a pedagogic and creative craftsman with just a touch of the naughty 'geezer' too.

Note

1   Patrick Reyntiens, 'Humour and Transcendence in Architecture', *AA Files*, no 10, 1985.

Industrial baroque

Nigel Coates and NATØ

During the mid-1980s, interior design, product design and, to a lesser extent, architecture, were susceptible to what I shall call 'detritus chic'. A cynic might argue that the taste of the middle classes for rust, flame-cut steel, shattered glass and hybrid, garbage items, could be a bourgeois affectation that conceals its guilt and the terror of a disaffected working class. At this time, some of the great bastions of the working class were being eroded. The power of the unions was in question and unemployment ravaged the inner cities; social unrest was rife and exploded into frequent riots. A few, including Ron Arad with his rusty, crude and vaguely beautiful 'one-off' shop; Danny Lane and his cracked glass tables and sculpture; and Tom Dixon's readymade eclectic ballcock and wrought-iron winged chairs, caught the *Zeitgeist*. Perhaps the greatest influence on this trend was Nigel Coates and the NATØ (Narrative Architecture Today) group. Coates was Unit Master of Diploma Unit 10 at the Architectural Association in London. His concerns were not merely aesthetic. He threw his unit against the political backdrop of urban decline, the demise of manufacturing industry and the loss of self-respect of the working class. His students investigated and proposed whole urban areas from the Isle of Dogs in East London and up through the dismal hinterland of Waterloo Station and County Hall in the centre of town.

ArkAlbion, 1984.

100

Industrial baroque
Nigel Coates and NATØ

The Cathedral 2000.

Before this happened, in early 1983, the AA held an exhibition of the work of Unit 10 over its ten year history, first under Bernard Tschumi and then onwards from 1979 under Nigel Coates. It contained some of the early works by the members of NATØ, which was yet to be fully formed. Some of its polemic protocols, however, were already visible. In the forward to the accompanying catalogue, *The Discourse of Events*, Alvin Boyarsky, then Chairman of the AA, attempted to put into words the unit's design imperative:

> The starting point for the unit was the programme, particularly as
> seen from the point of view of the individuals involved. Inevitably,
> this led to spatial interpretations more closely allied to the space of
> literature, films and performance than to traditional architectural
> modes, a corresponding development of notational systems, in situ
> experiments, appropriate graphic systems, special sympathy for the
> actions and life of some of the shabby but vital urban institutions of
> the moment and more recently at a synthesis at city scale, based on
> the grim economic realities of our time.[1]

In the same catalogue, at the end of his piece 'Narrative Break-Up', Coates is more expressively upbeat as he hints at the full-blown NATØ proposals yet to come:

> This *narrative architecture* grows out of an elaborate combination,
> piling all these things on top of each other, so that in terms of actual

effect, the narrative breaks up, like interference on a video screen . . .
Everything you do there is touched by the resonant effects of ordinary
things . . . reality becomes a screen of bursting little flames of light
through which you can just make out the next episode in the unit's
activity, *Albion* the art/science city threading its way from Surrey
Docks across Rotherhithe and Bermondsey right up to London Bridge.[2]

In October 1984, the exhibition spaces of the AA were infiltrated by ArkAlbion,
an urban proposal for South London that haemorrhaged, over the floor, up the
walls and even on the ceiling. It was with ArkAlbion that Coates and NATØ started
to articulate fully their urban and aesthetic concerns and proclivities.

Coates declared:

> ArkAlbion's site is full of large institutional buildings that have
> outlived their form, like Waterloo, St Thomas's and Lambeth Palace.
> Between them lie viaducts, wastelands and motorised deserts. It is
> amongst all this that ArkAlbion proposes a living exhibition in which
> the public can witness the fusing of office, factory, shop, home, into
> one volatile city fibre.
>
> To get there, ArkAlbion starts with what it finds idiosyncratic and
> paces through a design process which oscillates between overt
> pragmatism and outright absurdity. Then form and programme are
> worked up together to generate a constant edge of instability amongst
> the clearest possible signposts. Like the Festival of Britain, its
> architecture is public, episodic and persuasive; unlike it, the last
> thing it wants is one story, one building. It does this with six new
> functional bands that forge their way through the site, each one
> mutating along its length, so that say, the offices adjacent to
> Waterloo adopt medical functions, while further along the same band,
> St Thomas's Hospital fixes computer work stations between the beds
> . . . – industrial Baroque.[3]

After ArkAlbion, urban design had changed forever.

The following year, 'Gamma City' was exhibited. If ArkAlbion was NATØ's urbanity,
then 'Gamma City' was its agit-prop products – products that attempted to catch
the distorted dynamics of stylistic profusion. These pieces rejoiced in the fecun-
dity, entropy and surrealism of industrial consumer culture. Brian Hatton provides
us with a succinct description of the approach of 'Gamma City', which was exhibited in London's Air Gallery from November to December 1985:

ArkAlbion, 1984.

Space is not contained by rational containment and division: it is enacted and transformed by deed and narrative, tools and props. The Gamma show was an exhibition of such *produkti* mutating in the radioactive rain forest of post-industrial culture. The rain is man-made (one of the Gamma *produkti* was a surgical shower, the equivalent of gamma rays). 'Why Gamma?' wrote Nigel Coates in the third issue of *NATØ* magazine accompanying the show. 'Because gamma-rays emit spontaneously . . . affecting built mutations.'[4]

In 'Gamma', one was surrounded by objects that almost bit back. These NATØ pieces and their vast urban freeform prescriptions were in political terms having their cake and eating it. These were *laissez faire* developments yet articulated to a capitalist market; they attempted to be liberal yet brought the toil of work deep and heavily into the home, their anarchic vitality based on the shabbiness of garbage and its momentary art-gallery chic. However, one admires a valiant attempt to reconstruct the Western city and to lay bare its foibles and idiosyncrasies, for here is where dreams are forged and the future made.

Notes

1   'The Discourse of Events', *Themes 3*, Architectural Association, 1983.

2   Ibid.

3   Brian Hatton, 'Produkti for Metamorpolis', *Architectural Association Files*, no 12, 1986.

4   Ibid.

Spinoza's Garden. A series of
pottery pieces set out in a
grid juxtaposed with other
pottery vessels to convey its
symbolic sense.

Particles and sedimentality

Raoul Bunschoten

Raoul Bunschoten is one of an elite coterie of students who studied with Daniel Libeskind at Cranbrook Academy in the early 1980s. This group included Ben Nicholson, Don Bates, Karl Chu, Bahram Shirdel, Hal Leassig and Jesse Reiser. Between them, they created a body of work that was both highly creative and intellectually experimental. Much of the work encouraged at Cranbrook would not have been tolerated in more mundane and prosaic schools of architecture; one must applaud Libeskind for battling the forces of mediocrity.

Bunschoten is recognised as a thinker and maker of poetic and polemical projects. Latterly, he has formed CHORA – an organisation interested in developing new strategies of urban and cultural rejuvenation, but it is his early work that interests us here. In a text written to support his work at Cranbrook, Bunschoten declares some of the themes that have preoccupied him for two decades and continue to serve him well. These include the landscape, with its detrital deposition and subtle movement; time; the alchemic transmutation of matter as an analogy for creative and epistemological thought; and a love of the phenomenology of materials and the way they are pulled from the earth. The piece is entitled 'To begin with there is the thing':

> There is always something dusty and fossilic about the thing, it pretends to be real, yet it is only the sediment of the process of construction or what is left behind after the idea of the thing. It holds us down, binds us to the Earth. It connects us with the physical aspects of the world, the tactile qualities. We make it, we make it of something, this something is not ourselves, it is in the other material. We make it with purpose, the purpose is us, we determine it, we want it. So it carries our determinations, its purposefulness is the essence, not that it is, but that it leads to some goal. The essence of its purposefulness is embodied by the materials it is constructed with . . .[1]

The projects I wish to highlight here are 'Spinoza's Garden' and 'Apieron', both made in the mid-1980s, after Cranbrook and before CHORA. Spinoza's Garden was the result of an invitation to exhibit work at the Architecture Biennale in

This page and opposite: Spinoza's Garden.

Holland. It is based on the dynamics, essence, strange metamorphosis, ambience and memory of the Dutch polder. In 1986, Bunchoten described the work:

> A polder is land that is reclaimed from the sea. Part of the sea is girdled with dikes and its covering of water pumped into the surrounding sea, a process that can take up to nine months. A world of silt remains – wet, uneven, punctuated by drowned sunken objects such as ships or planes with their contents scattered around them. Reeds are sown from the air, which form a sea of swaying tops. The reeds dehydrate the soil. The newly exposed objects disappear again among the stems of the reeds and wildflowers. Large cracks appear, insects arrive, birds begin to nest. The urban development, which follows, is a sad example of fast internal colonisation. The 'pristine' land is covered with an infrastructure borrowed from its surroundings, its purpose being to achieve the utmost economic and social efficiency.

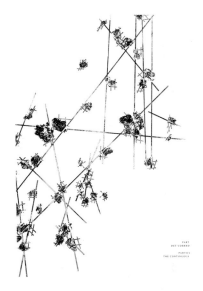

The purpose embodied in 'Spinoza's Garden' was once regarded as the transmutation of matter: water evaporates, clay solidifies, and earth is given form. In the final transmutation, fire, stone and air are for a brief moment animated. Incandescence and incineration is an intermittent process, luminosity and purified (and therefore partly translucent) residue its product.

The Garden represents the growth of Spinoza's animated matter: 'A forest of lofty thoughts whose flowering tops sway while the immovable trunks are rooted in the eternal earth' (Heinrich Heine on Spinoza). Cosmological meaning has traditionally been expressed in a garden by using nature to represent an abstract order; Spinoza's abstract world represents growth inversely. The traditional garden familiarises mental or physical reflections of what is outside of it, whereas 'Spinoza's Garden' reflects intimacy. This, however, cannot be 'known', nor can it be entered, a distinction which can be illustrated by comparing a Byzantine church to a Zen garden. Like a sphere in the hand, which contains more space than earth and sky together, it encompasses everything but excludes access by any means save contemplation.[2]

'Apieron' consists of a series of cuts in a roughly textured monolithic place. Suspended above the figured ground are objects, particles strung on wires – all of which are contained in a square frame, games of void and mass, macro mass and macro void. The particles, whilst reminding one of fresh liver against Ronchamp's walls, are also figured – not pure. Here is architecture's *prima materia* – the tools of our trade, laid out, laid bare, here for all to see, simple yet astoundingly beautiful in their fundamental essence. 'Apieron' is an object of contemplation, a spatial mandala, the universe in a loose-fitting frame. Its compositional adhesive seems to be a type of fluctuating gravity gradient that can be turned up to produce clusters of forms, materials and lines.

Apieron.

Bunschoten's projects are directly related to Libeskind's groundbreaking work, but Bunschoten's is more sculptural and revels in the tactility and forming of materials. So few architects work at this

Apieron. In essence a steel frame supporting a caste concrete tablet. Stretched across the frame is a series of particles and cuttings on the surface.

level, or seek a synthesis between the meaning of architecture, philosophical discourse and pure creativity that challenges the viewer. Such work is extremely important to the continued vitality of architecture as a yardstick with which to view and explore the world.

Notes

1   Raoul Bunschoten, 'Work of Cranbrook Studio', *Parametro*, no 119, August-September 1983.

2   Raoul Bunschoten, 'Spinoza's Garden', *AA Files*, no 11, 1986.

Tomorrow's think tank today

Andrew Birds

View from adjoining cliffs.
Tomorrow's Think Tank
Today, 1984.

In 1984, the Royal Institute of British Architects instigated a series of yearly international open competitions for students. The first assessment and brief-writing panel consisted of Sir Clive Sinclair, Norman Foster and Ted Happold. A brief was written and it was agreed that each competitor could choose their own site. The brief was to design a research institute for Sinclair, at the time a celebrity, the toast of industry for his visionary, High-tech entrepreneurism. His company had marketed some of the first calculators, watches and computers, and he was also the creator of the notorious C5 three-wheel electric car. Little is heard of him today. Foster's technological and aesthetic preoccupations need no introduction. Happold was Professor of Building Engineering at the University of Bath and the principal of the engineering office Buro Happold. He was part of a triumvirate of engineers (the others were Peter Rice and Tony Hunt) connected to the High-tech masters, whose specialities included tension structures. (Putting aside for a moment the machinations of the postmodernists, the 1980s was the decade of the structural engineer. They assumed the same celebrity status as their soon-to-be-knighted and ennobled High-tech architect friends.)

For this first competition, one could expect an eclectic series of projects from architectural students from around the world. Many would seize on the gaudy, colour-coded, technologised language towards which the judges seemed to be sympathetic. Others would deliver postmodern pedimented narratives. Still others might have some success with the sort of well-mannered English Modernism prevalent at the Bartlett School, Bath and Cambridge – the sort that makes me spit blood, swear and curse, gripped in the throes of suicidal boredom. All these classes of solution to the brief featured in the exhibition and the awards roster.

110

Tomorrow's think tank today
Andrew Birds

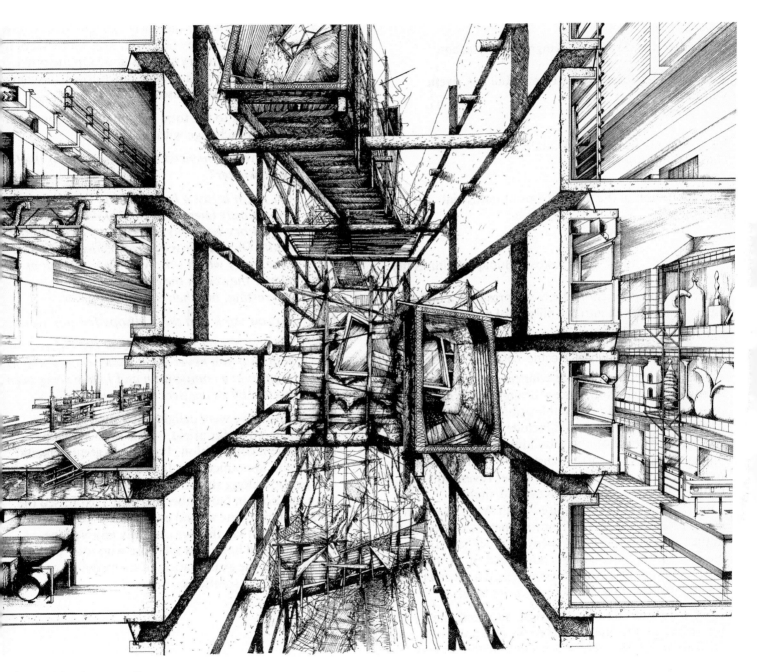

Sectional interior perspective.

Vignettes.

The first prizewinner, however, was Andrew Birds, with a quite extraordinary project. '[It] conforms to no ideological preconceptions', wrote a slightly taken aback Peter Davy, Editor of the *Architectural Review*, in the July issue.

> It was undoubtedly one of the most original entries, and one of the best drawn. It was also the one with the strongest feeling for place (a small bay in Kent). But it is difficult to see how, divided into two virtually unconnected rectangles, it could be an economical workplace. Or that anyone would really like to work there, for its penitentiary-like blocks face each other across a chasm of flotsam containing the relics of temporary experiments and see far too little of the sea. And (curiously in a design chosen by Foster and Happold) it seems quite unbuildable as it is drawn. Yet it does, of course, provide an absolutely unforgettable image – which is why Sinclair put it first on his list.

One had seen nothing like it. The initial shock and incredulity swiftly became interest and then fascination. Norman Foster, in the same issue of *AR*, described the project:

In this scheme two man-made cliffs of laboratories are inserted into the rock of a coastline separated by a vertical void containing circulation. The laboratories are modules which appear as gargantuan building blocks articulated by glass strips. As a project, it could be read at several levels – a poetic allegory for instance, with its overtones of medieval alchemy, and a central space of disordered menace that with its driftwood imagery recalled Hieronymus Bosch or even John Wyndham's *Triffids*.

The chasms of flotsam and jetsam have a Libeskind-like dynamic reminiscent of the 'Chamberworks' series that had been exhibited at the Architectural Association the previous year. However, when one looks more closely at this accumulated detritus, it does not share Libeskind's abstraction or denial of codification, but is charged with memory, trace and patina. These pieces of driftwood, cut nets and lashed-together fences suggest an architecture in awe of the power of the sea and the terrible forces it is capable of unleashing. Are these really the wreckage of past experiments as Davy suggested? I think not; this is not High-tech garbage. Perhaps Birds found in his project and drawings a repository for some of the things that fascinated him yet were almost forbidden in the rarefied atmosphere of most architectural schools at that time.

Sketch view.

What Birds achieves that is so rare is the cunning juxtaposition of opposites. The project cleverly navigates the boundaries between the accidental and the considered, the pure and the broken, the narrative and the functional, and the crazy and the sane. The drawings themselves hark back to an era of frenzied etching, evoking foreboding shadows and the lurking dangers of wind and vertigo. Birds' chosen method of representation and composition in the drawings is the simple plan of the laboratories contrasting with the detrital abyss. Plan views are collaged in an almost deconstructivist way. Perspectives are arranged on the sheet so that the normative placement of individual views relies on the internal dynamics of each perspective for theatrical effect.

The project's audacity sticks in the mind because of its combination of the sublime with the almost naïve. For me, it was another signal that architecture was at the beginning of a Renaissance, was becoming much more idiosyncratic, inventive and sometimes downright naughty. It was a glimpse beyond the humble sparseness of the Cambridge School or the hippy high jinks of the do-anything-anywhere-anytime-with-a-balloon crowd. It caused a bit of a tizz at the time.

Catalytic iconoclasm

Alsop and Lyall

National Gallery Extension, London, 1982.

During the early to mid-1980s, Will Alsop and John Lyall, ex-students of the Architectural Association and graduates of Cedric Price's office, emerged on the architectural skyline. Their projects were bad-mannered, stylistically eclectic and highly unusual. These included the Riverside Arts complex in Hammersmith (1982) and the National Gallery extension in Trafalgar Square (1982). Both schemes were unlikely combinations of forms, fenestration and architectural conceit. They helped forge Alsop and Lyall's reputation for iconoclastic thinking, originality and a devil-may-care attitude.

Unlike many of the proposals for the National Gallery extension, which displayed a conservationist shyness and a reactionary, classical approach, Alsop and Lyall would have no truck with the heart-of-the-British-Empire site. Their wild facade,

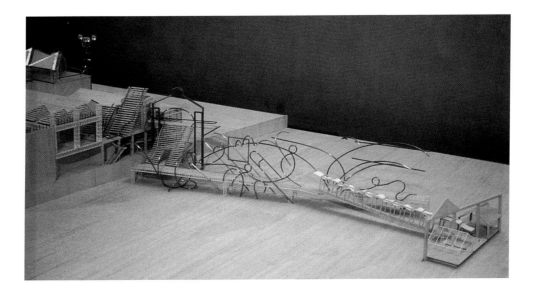

Above and right: Riverside
Studios, Hammersmith,
London, 1982.

which had some affinity with Goodheart-Rendell's Hays Wharf at London Bridge, showed no aspiration to imperial correctness. As is often the case in the British architectural competition system, a debacle followed. The Prince of Wales jumped in with his own brand of architectural criticism and the lowest common denominator of Robert Venturi's Sainsbury Wing resulted.

Around this time, something cataclysmic happened at Alsop and Lyall: they began to explore sites and ideas through large, drippy paintings. Though these had always been used by the team (which included Jonathan Adams, also featured in this book), now they became a fundamental tool and client presentation device. These brightly coloured paintings, beautiful but with a child-like crudity, were published in the *Architectural Review*, illustrating proposals for Hamburg's City Centre (1985).

Above and left: Riverside
Studios, Hammersmith,
London, 1982.

This scheme, spatially and programmatically skilled, consists of movable roofs, walkways, hybrid programmes and catalytic structures aimed at encouraging users to do something different. Though unfortunately it was never built, this was the genesis of much that was to come later. The building-as-catalyst idea became a watchword in Alsop and Lyall's gaudily coloured world.

While working with Cedric Price, the partners had become interested in his view that architecture is an expedient, enabling tool. The notion of catalytic action in their work was centred on the belief that if one could set up a process of change, colonisation and recolonisation, architecture could have a longer life-cycle and could be more effective in facilitating and attracting other proposals and strategies to a previously defunct area.

Below: Hamburg City Centre, 1984–5. Interior paintings.

Alsop and Lyall were also pioneers of a more collaborative architectural practice, often working with dancers, choreographers, artists and sculptors, such as Bruce McClean and Gareth Jones. Their practice was much more akin to an artist's studio than to an architect's office. Its products were therefore more recognisable as the creative residues of intense artistic speculation – alive and vital. In 1996, Alsop contributed to *Architectural Design*'s 'Integrating Architecture' issue with an essay entitled 'The Context for Practice', which underlines this aspect of his approach:

> Robert Irwin, the American artist has, for me, always been a relevant source of reference. His identification of separate frames of reference as a context for art practice can equally apply to architecture. I substitute ARCHITECTURE for ART:

> 1 ARCHITECTURE is a positive of aesthetic enquiry the perceptual/conceptual recognition, construction and individual ordering of individual reality. ARCHITECTURE as ARCHITECTURE.

> 2 ARCHITECTURE is a process of cultural innovation, through interdisciplinary articulation and argumentation by means of which novel ideas and forms achieve cultural validity. The ARCHITECTURE of ARCHITECTURE.

> 3 ARCHITECTURE is a communicative interaction with social need, the fostering of those 'meaningful' overlaps of form for social practice and function. The ARCHITECTURE of SOCIAL CONCERN.

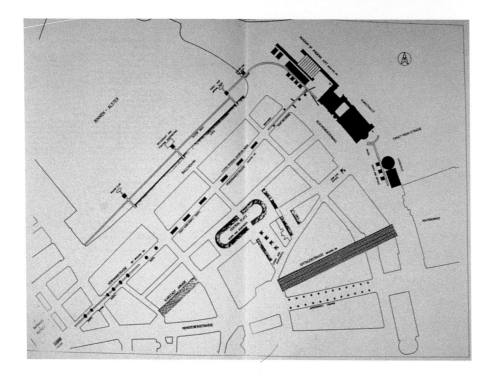

Hamburg City Centre,
1984–5. Above: Site plan;
right: interior prospective
and interior paintings.

Hamburg City Centre, 1984–5.

4 ARCHITECTURE is a compounded historical development. This historical process is the grounds for art as a sophisticated cultural discipline. The ARCHITECTURE of CIVILISATION.[1]

Latterly, Alsop and Lyall have gone their separate ways, both fronting their own successful practices. Each continues to pioneer expeditions into the more off-road terrain of architectural practice.

Seeing these projects again brings back the tingling, visceral thrill of viewing them for the first time. Alsop and Lyall made a massive contribution to the way in which architectural practice was conducted in the 1990s, both in terms of stylistic touches and, more importantly, in demonstrating how architecture can be catalytic, an agent of beneficial effect over a long, ever-changing period of time.

Notes

1   William Alsop, 'The Context of Practice', in Neil Spiller (ed), 'Integrating Architecture', *Architectural Design*, no 123, 1996.

Making the invisible visible

Allford Hall Monaghan Morris

AHMM was formed in 1989. The partners (Simon Allford, Jonathan Hall, Peter Morris, Paul Monaghan) are all graduates from the Bartlett School of Architecture, University College, London. AHMM is not known for its experimental work, but for good-quality, light-fingered Modernism. Its work is mostly in response to commission and is rarely speculative. Its architectural dreams are often masked in the *Spiel* of developers and clients, but that is not to say that they are any the less imaginative. There have been occasions on which the considered cloak slips and speculation and polemic are revealed. This undercurrent in AHMM's work has always been there and was even evident before the official foundation of the practice.

In 1987, Simon Allford, then an architect working for the London office of BDP, won a *Building Design*/British Steel ideas competition for the rejuvenation of Brighton's West Pier. It is an elemental design whose success rests on the composition of pieces that respond to wave, tide and wind to create a menu of spaces

West Pier, Brighton, 1987.

West Pier, Brighton, 1987.

to bathe, sunbathe, watch and play. Along with a glass-walled swimming pool is a second pool

with a buoyant concrete wall that floats on the surface. Open grilles at each end allow in waves and small fish while keeping out unwelcome visitors such as sharks, which are not unknown off the south coast. A jogging track is slung beneath the main deck. This will allow joggers to exercise without bumping into people and otherwise annoying day-trippers. An automatically adjusting skydiving platform . . . will move up and down in response to the tide so that swimmers will always have a guaranteed height from which to dive . . . a jetty for anglers, a wave research station . . . A 300 feet high tower at the end of the pier giving views to France.[1]

Paternoster Square, London,
1986. Conceptual project.

This was the *Sunday Times* architecture critic Hugh Pearman's description of the project. In the same article, he quotes Simon Allford:

> The idea is that you should return to the experience of the sea. Piers used to be quite lively places but they lost their way. You could call this a bit of a purist concept, but it would be great fun to go to. There would still be a place for candy floss and whelk stalls on the restored section.

AHMM is sometimes prone to graphic polemic. Its 'scheme' for London's Paternoster Square by St Paul's Cathedral (1996) is a critique, explored through a series of collages, of planning densities and their erratic changes over the previous few decades. It was an idea aimed directly at the heart of mealy-mouthed planners and the conservationist lobby. The images are still popular with the practice, and hint at another side of AHMM — one with iconoclastic leanings.

AHMM's most flamboyant projects are always buildable without waiting for an idealised future, a change of economic constraints or a new technology. Such a project is the unbuilt glass house on the Isle of Skye (1990), which became a crucial PR image for the 'New Architects Show', held in 1994 at London's Architectural Foundation — an institution that seldom pushes the envelope of architecture. The house was all glass and was designed in conjunction with structural engineers Dewhurst McFarlane. Hugh Pearman, in a later issue of the *Sunday Times*, wrote of it:

Isle of Skye, Glass House, 1994.   Isle of Skye, Glass House, 1994. Interior.

. . . the glass house is perfectly feasible. Nor, these days, is it always transparent, unless you want it to be. Glass can be structural – even supporting beams can be made of the material. It can hold the heat in, and bounce unwanted sun back out . . . You can turn it from clear to opaque at the flick of a switch, using technology derived from flat computer screens.

The house would have been populated by brightly coloured glass functional mechanisms – bathroom, bedroom, kitchen study and wine cellar – which would have moved around like furniture.[2]

In recent years, AHMM has been more successful than most and is now an established part of the British architectural institution. The practice has had little time to spend on polemic and speculation, but its competition work has not suffered: it wins more often than not. With a safe work flow now under its belt, it is to be hoped that it further develops its iconoclastic side towards even more sublime propositions.

Notes

1   Hugh Pearman, 'On the crest of a new wave', *Sunday Times*, 19 July 1987.

2   Hugh Pearman, 'I have a little plan', *Sunday Times*, 24 April 1994.

Liquid landscapes

Jonathan Adams

Jonathan Adams' 'Water Park' project (1988) has stuck in my mind for over ten years, a Diploma student assignment set by Peter Cook at the Architectural Association in London. Here, he recounts some of the thoughts and aspirations behind it:

> The site is the stretch of the south bank from Bankside Power Station eastwards, passing beneath (and incorporating) Southwark Bridge and ending just west of London Bridge.

> The only edges that concerned me were the interface with the river, and the interlinking of the body of Southwark Bridge to the roof of the largest building, the central leisure/competition swimming pool. There were two entrance areas: one at the west end, where there was a sort of information centre (referred to as the Head Building), and the other off Southwark Bridge.

> The remains of Bankside Power Station are used for car parking. There is a sort of paddy-field or water garden making up the space between the Thames and the old Power Station. All the way along, the edge to the river is indefinite.

> The three circular filtration beds shown on the Head Building isometric are the reused oil tanks from Bankside Power Station. The Head Building was conceived as a kind of perpetual torrent. Water would gush from beneath it in a thunderous white-water explosion and flow from there at various speeds along the waterways in the eastward direction. The water was to be drawn from the Thames, cleaned and propelled through the Water Park around and within the wide-span building with the shallow, curved glass roof.

> The Head Building has a visitor's section (illustrated in the long-section drawing with all the odd-shaped stairs) and a

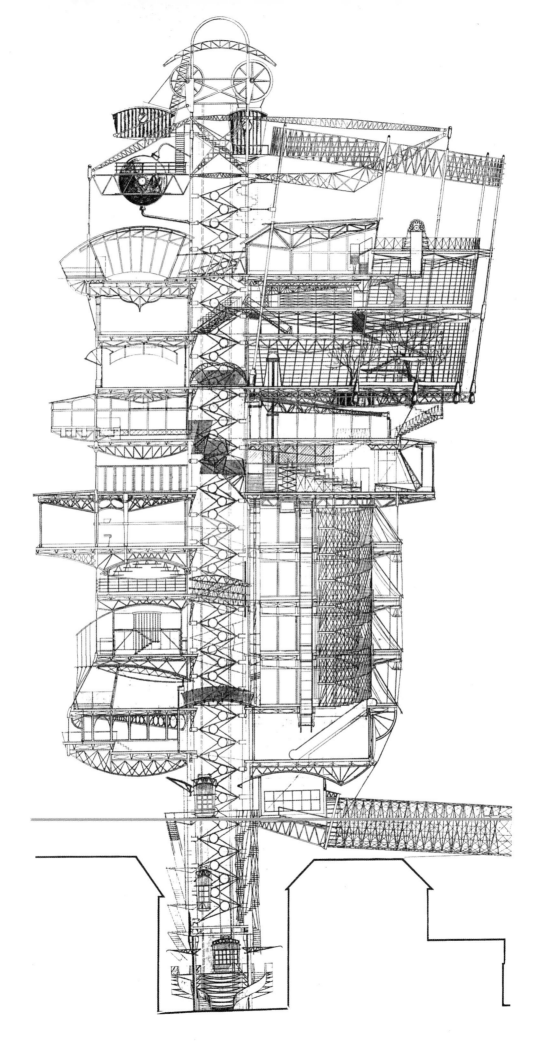

Liquid landscapes
Jonathan Adams

Head Building, Water Park,
1988. Section.

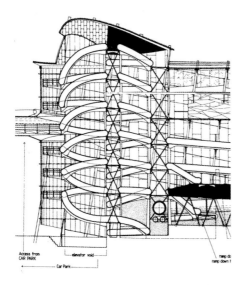

pump-house/water-treatment section. The big pipe that draws water into the building from the Thames runs into the complex directly beneath the building. This is a clear reference to the Ludwig Leo building in Berlin, with the big bent pipe underneath it. I remember that in the mid-1980s, it was very frustrating to feel that one was expected to take either one side or the other of the great modern versus postmodern debate. Like many of my contemporaries, I yearned for something that was neither the one nor the other, but which was individual, distinctive and conveyed someone's individual imagination. The Ludwig Leo building was a real touchstone. There are some other ideas in the visitors' building that I like: the windows with fish in-between the double glazing; the bar that looks like a stickleback nest; the pipe/foot-tunnel leading under the river.

The watercourses that flow away from the Head Building combine aquaculture with people-use. The southernmost is an angling river, stocked for fly-fishing etc. Then there's a trout farm, which takes the form of a continuous fast-moving river along a series of weirs. The next one is the swimming river, which is like a cresta run for swimming, going from indoors to out and above ground to underground etc. Again, this has a continuous west-to-east flow, to carry you from the Head Building down to the main pool. Next to that is a series of tanks for aquaculture of shellfish and eels. Lastly, alongside the river and separated from it only by a flexible sheet-steel wall is an underwater diving facility

The most interesting area (for me at least) is that around Southwark Bridge. I proposed making provision for the majority of visitors to enter the complex by coming down off the bridge. The big building for which the bridge forms part of the roof is the main swimming-pool and diving-pool building. This is entered and controlled via three other buildings, each of which meets the bridge with an entrance off it. These three buildings all sit on top of the concrete piers that support the bridge and then extend out to carry the building on top. I like this idea very much.

Liquid landscapes
Jonathan Adams

I worked hard to make the architecture personal to me. I remember suffering the typically turbulent social life of the student at the time, and that particular period was one of fairly intense peaks and troughs. I remember thinking that I had to get some of that feeling into the design and into the drawings. I think the drawings and the design both have a sort of Gothic romanticism, which, for me, is very evocative of that time of my life.

Technically, I was trying to be fairly adventurous. I was enraptured by techniques of forming and joining metals. I learned to weld to quite a high standard. I enjoyed making sculptural things in reinforced concrete. I loved mechanical fixings. It seemed to me that with these methods you should be able to build *anything*.

Will Alsop [his tutor at intermediate level] often talked about disarticulating elements, so that each part of an assemblage was individually expressed and fitted into a hierarchy. I felt instinctively (and still do) that it was better to work the other way: to design the building so that, for example, the shower partitions were also the primary super-structure. It was essential to me that every part also carried a bit of the overall pattern or rhythm of the building. I think people like feeling that they are inhabiting a *sculpture*, rather than a functional assemblage of bits. This is why I detest talk of 'architectural integrity' in the modernist sense. To me, the only integrity worth bothering with is artistic integrity, the honest expression of *ideas*.

Drawing itself was obviously a sensual pleasure, and a pain. Therapeutic and tortuous. It was a discipline like no other.
I was afraid to give it up because I thought that it was my professional strength.
But I now realise that one good idea is worth a hundred good drawings, and that the computer is, if not a friend, then at least at lot less physically exhausting than the t-square and adjustable.

Below and opposite: Water Park, 1988. Below: overall axonometric. Opposite, from the top: Sections and axonometric.

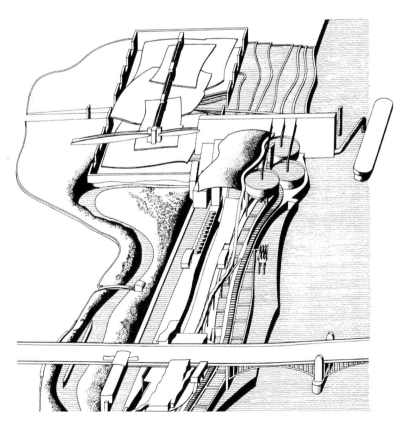